"Beautiful. Magnetic. True. Danny touches your heart and the heart of God as he recounts this unwanted journey through his deepest valley. Young love, young children, and a young musical career intertwine to express God's mysterious shaping of spiritual lives in a world filled with joy and pain."

— JERRY WHITE

president, The Navigators

"Our stories are important. They remind us of what we have in common and how different we can be. Some are easier to tell than others. Danny cares enough to tell us his hard and beautiful story and in the process remind us that just as Jesus has cared for and carried him, He will do the same for us."

— GEOFF MOORE

contemporary Christian recording artist

Mommy PAINTS THE Sky

A LOVE STORY

DANNY OERTLI

NAVPRESS®

BRINGING TRUTH TO LIFE

OUR GUARANTEE TO YOU

We believe so strongly in the message of our books that we are making this quality guarantee to you. If for any reason you are disappointed with the content of this book, return the title page to us with your name and address and we will refund to you the list price of the book. To help us serve you better, please briefly describe why you were disappointed. Mail your refund request to: NavPress, P.O. Box 35002, Colorado Springs, CO 80935.

The Navigators is an international Christian organization. Our mission is to reach, disciple, and equip people to know Christ and to make Him known through successive generations. We envision multitudes of diverse people in the United States and every other nation who have a passionate love for Christ, live a lifestyle of sharing Christ's love, and multiply spiritual laborers among those without Christ.

NavPress is the publishing ministry of The Navigators. NavPress publications help believers learn biblical truth and apply what they learn to their lives and ministries. Our mission is to stimulate spiritual formation among our readers.

ISBN 1-57683-688-6

Cover design by UDG/DesignWorks, Inc.
Cover photo by photos.com, Veer, and PhotoDisk
Creative Team: Dan Rich, Rachelle Gardner, Arvid Wallen, Darla Hightower, Glynese Northam

Some of the anecdotal illustrations in this book are true to life and are included with the permission of the persons involved. All other illustrations are composites of real situations, and any resemblance to people living or dead is coincidental.

Unless otherwise identified, all Scripture quotations in this publication are taken from the HOLY BIBLE: NEW INTERNATIONAL VERSION® (NIV®). Copyright © 1973, 1978, 1984 by International Bible Society. Used by permission of Zondervan Publishing House. All rights reserved.

Published in association with David Lipscomb of Overflow, Inc., P.O. Box 218, Franklin, TN 37065.

Oertli, Danny, 1971-
    Mommy paints the sky : a love story / Danny Oertli.
      p. cm.
    Includes bibliographical references (p.   ).
    ISBN 1-57683-688-6
    1. Consolation. 2. Bereavement--Religious aspects--Christianity. 3. Oertli,
Danny, 1971--Religion. 4. Oertli, Cyndi.   I. Title.
BV4905.3.O47 2004
248.8′66′0922--dc22
[B]
                                                    2004015265

Printed in Canada

FOR A FREE CATALOG OF
NAVPRESS BOOKS & BIBLE STUDIES,
CALL 1-800-366-7788 (USA)
OR 1-416-499-4615 (CANADA)

For Grace and Jack

Live For Heaven!

Contents

So we fix our eyes not on what is seen, but on what is unseen. For what is seen is temporary, but what is unseen is eternal.

2 CORINTHIANS 4:18

Prologue

THE WIND BLEW COLD THROUGH THE PINE TREES THAT LINED THE deserted road. I have always loved the way the mountains make the evening sky turn purple as dusk approaches. But this night, the stars haunted me.

I heard the lonely crunch of tires rolling over gravel as I slowed the car to a stop, then I opened the door and walked across the deserted road. The quiet of February rested upon the mountains but a roar of pain was growing within my chest. Looking to the stillness and majesty of the hills for comfort I found only the breath of the wind. My feet slid on the rocks as I climbed my way to the top of the small hill overlooking the valley.

Cyndi had hiked these hills as a girl, and we once had dreamed of building a house in these high mountain meadows, lush with the crisp scent of cold pine. But as I stood looking across the valley, those dreams seemed impossibly long ago. I wrapped my arms around myself and shivered in the wind, watching the darkness fall and wondering what I had been looking for the past two hours.

I had driven by her childhood home just down the road, but she wasn't there. Somehow in my desperation, I had felt that I might hear her laughter in the wind or sense her presence in these mountains of our youth and early love. But I heard no voice and felt no ghost. Instead of finding some solace in reminiscence, I felt completely and utterly alone. The pain of fear was in my chest, only this was not a fleeting blow; its intensity had remained for more than a week, crushing me.

How could I possibly face a future so hopeless, so void of purpose? What was I doing here in these hills? What was I looking for? Where was God? Why did Cyndi have to die? Pain and emptiness swallowed me. I felt overcome and undone in every way.

Then in the silence, something whispered. As I heard the secret that was revealed to me, I fell to my knees and knew my life would never be the same.

Cyndi and I, dressed for the 1987 Colorado Springs Christian School Banquet.

The Smile
(FIFTEEN YEARS EARLIER)

FALL WAS SWEEPING ITS WAY FROM THE HIGH ROCKY MOUNTAIN PASSES down to vast plains covered in shimmering yellow aspens. The trunks of the great trees groaned against the wind as their leaves crackled in harmony, one by one giving up their hold on summer.

In the gathering shadow of Pikes Peak, I quickly flipped a basketball between my hands to warm my fingers. Larry Bird's signature had nearly worn away from countless hours of being beaten against the pitted driveway. Often the monotonous bounce of the ball had provoked the neighbors to complain. But like many teenagers, I had learned just how far I could push before the calls started coming.

I strained my ears to listen. There was the faint sound of a telephone ringing inside the house. With just a few quick strides, I flung open the garage door, raced up the five steps into the kitchen, and picked up the phone. My friend Erik's voice was easy to recognize; I had spent countless hours on the basketball court with him. He invited me to join him and his girlfriend, Erin, at a progressive dinner for a local church youth group. I didn't have to think about it twice. The Colorado

Springs community was small in those days, and I was sure to see a few friends from my Christian high school. Now a sixteen-year-old sophomore, I had earned my driver's license only a few weeks before and welcomed any excuse to get out of the house and meet friends.

Amazingly, I had little trouble starting the car: a white 1979 Ford Pinto complete with red racing stripes. Life as a pastor's kid was full of surprises, and one of the least delightful to me had been my car. It was without question the ugliest and least reliable vehicle in my school, possibly in the city. In true adolescent form, my friends and I had named it "Satan" in an attempt to make light of the grievous situation. After only a few weeks, the car was a legend. We'd even installed a horn that played 99 different tunes to announce our triumphant arrival at events.

That night, I made the twenty-minute drive north from Colorado Springs to Monument, a small community nestled against the foothills. I parked behind the cars that lined the dirt road in front of the first house on the evening's itinerary. Feeling good, I played a particularly merry song on my car horn to herald my entrance.

I felt slightly disconcerted when I failed to recognize a familiar face in all of those peering my way. I quickly found Erik. We exchanged the timeless, wordless greeting of teenage boys — a nod — and made our way into the house. Laughing my way through the entryway and down the stairs, I arrived at the bottom just in time to see *it*. It was brief, but unmistakable, like the flash of gold in a pan or the brilliant strike of lightning across the night sky . . . yes, there it was again. Bubbling, then resurfacing. I hadn't come looking for such a thing; in fact, I had never even thought it could exist. But there it was: simply the most beautiful, sincere, inviting smile I had ever seen.

The girl attached to the smile was laughing with a friend while dishing up bowls of ice cream; the combination of the two — girl plus ice cream — was practically the picture of heaven to my young eyes. I marveled at how arms so thin could wield the iron of an ice cream scoop. I suppressed a laugh as I watched her shift and move around the bucket of ice cream to gain leverage against her adversary. Her short hair was a mixture of brown and blond. She was average in height and very thin, with an almost girlish build. But it was her enthusiasm that drew me in. She was sparkling, effervescent. She seemed almost to dance with joy and happiness.

Circling the table from a distance, I made a pathetic attempt to watch her without overtly watching her. I talked with friends but was distracted by her presence. From a corner of the room, the event's youth pastor announced the beginning of an ice cream-eating contest. As if directed by God, or a finely tuned sense of woman's intuition, Erin walked me over to The Smile's table to introduce us. I learned that her name was Cyndi. Immediately, I felt the full enchantment of those laughing hazel eyes. I might have stood there indefinitely if the contest hadn't begun. To my amazement, we were suddenly partners.

At roughly five foot eleven and 155 pounds, *primed* would be a woefully inadequate way to describe my readiness for the task. At five foot five and 108 pounds, my teammate could only be described as *unprepared*. When the horn sounded, one of us was to feed the other for an allotted time, then switch places at the signal. I went first and, thanks to my competitive nature and deep love for ice cream, devoured an ungodly amount of vanilla. When we were signaled to switch, Cyndi's face lit up with another smile and I had great difficulty forcing the ice cream into her laughing mouth. With one last desperate attempt, I tried to get the spoon into her smiling lips, but she burst forth with a loud laugh and the ice cream dribbled down her brown sweater onto the floor.

For one of the few times in my life, I didn't care that I had lost a contest. This girl fascinated me. She was so different, so unique, so genuine. It wasn't just the way she placed her hand on a person's arm while she was talking or the way she leaned back when she laughed; it was her genuine enthusiasm that caught me. She seemed to love life and life seemed to love her back. In less than ten minutes, I had become completely hooked.

That night, I had great difficulty sleeping. Somehow, within the walls of our small school I had overlooked this extraordinary girl. Perhaps it was because she was one year my senior. As I watched her Jeep Cherokee pull into the school parking lot the next day, I made up my mind to get to know her better.

In the following weeks, I took every opportunity to pass her in the crowded halls. I learned that she was the daughter of a prominent local doctor and that her mother was working on a doctorate in psychology. Cyndi was not only brilliant, she was also a cheerleader and, if the rumors were true, a pretty speedy typist. In keeping with her studious nature, she occasionally wore thin tortoise shell glasses that seemed to accessorize her intelligence. Every time her name was mentioned among friends, there appeared to be the trail of a fond memory lingering in the eyes of those listening. As I would learn in the years to come, Cyndi always elicited strong emotions among those who knew her.

Nearly a month after the "Battle of Vanilla," I had successfully worked my way into Cyndi's circle of friends. November arrived with a chill and the grass faded to yellow as leaves blew through the city. The year was 1987, and on November 8 the most popular rock band in the world came to Denver. Two weeks earlier, I had slept on the sidewalk overnight so that the next morning I could buy tickets for my friends and me to see the band U2 on their Joshua Tree Tour. I had been playing guitar for a year and my love for music was beginning to rival my passion for basketball.

I wandered the halls of the arena knowing that somewhere in the crowd of 16,000, Cyndi also was in attendance. Before long, I ran into a friend who knew where Cyndi and her friends were sitting. I arrived just in time and as U2 began, we were all together in the first row of the balcony. I managed to sneak in right next to Cyndi to watch the show, and I stood beside her nearly bursting with the feelings of young love. I made a point of singing with each song, hoping she would be impressed not only by my ability to carry a tune but also by my vast knowledge of the Irish rock band's lyrics. Every few moments she grabbed my arm and spoke into my ear, pointing out something she had observed in the hazy auditorium. As the intense light and sound bombarded our senses, I noticed a subtle change in her smile and knew our affection for one another was becoming more obvious. This was all so new to me. I had been attracted to different girls before but never like this. She seemed so perfect, so fun! I felt as if I didn't need to sleep or eat; I just wanted to be with her. Four days later my life changed forever.

A horn honked and I looked through the front window just in time to see a white Toyota Camry speed into the cul-de-sac in front of my house. I leaped down the front steps. The car's windows were tinted but I could tell it was full of passengers by the obvious weight on the car's frame and by the volume of the music. Why does music always get louder when more people are in the car?

I squeezed into the back seat and quickly assessed the situation. Earlier in the day, I had been invited to go bowling with Cyndi and some friends. Although it would have been interesting to watch Cyndi's skinny arms wrestle a bowling ball, I had my suspicions about what the evening would really hold. A gut feeling told me that Cyndi's friends had noticed a spark between us and wanted to move the process along. Those suspicions seemed to be confirmed as I looked into the five playfully guilty faces of those in the car. I took note as we turned the opposite direction of the bowling alley but just laughed and went along for the ride. I didn't care where we were headed, I was just happy to be with Cyndi. Thanks to the confines of the small car, she and I were sandwiched together between two other friends. After about fifteen minutes, we arrived at a park.

"I don't see any pins to knock down," I said.

Instead of laughter, I was greeted by an awkward silence as the car came to a slow stop. With knowing smiles, each member of the conspiracy walked away into the park, leaving Cyndi and me alone on the sidewalk.

We exchanged a quick glance before she turned her face away, hiding any evidence I may have seen in her eyes regarding her involvement in this setup.

By this time, the sun had been chased over the mountains by a brilliant November moon. Everything was still and soundless, the autumn air crisp and vibrant, as if in anticipation of some momentous event. The world seemed to glow in silver and white. Cyndi stood gazing the opposite direction, her face bathed in moonbeams. Slowly she turned back to look at me, her eyes wide and lustrous.

"What do you want to talk about?" she whispered demurely, enjoying the moment.

Lacking sufficient vocabulary for the situation, I gently kissed her. And the night gloriously floated into history.

Danny and Herbie the Wonder Dog.

Marty, Herbie,

AND THE NIGHT SKY

MY MOM MARTY WAS ALWAYS THE FAVORITE IN OUR HOUSE. MANY TIMES I wondered if my friends were actually coming to see me or if the lure of my mom's chocolate chip cookies, homemade caramel corn, and blind encouragement was what drew them. For years, our house had been a safe, inviting center for entertainment and hospitality.

Marty was the fourth of five children raised on a small farm in southern Minnesota. In contrast to her more serious older siblings, she was whimsical and light, irrationally optimistic. God designed her as a social butterfly. Never a caterpillar, she started out her life flying. She had no time for a cocoon; that would have meant time away from the party. As a girl, she often risked the wrath of the local Baptist preacher, her father, by slipping through the window late at night to join Elvis in the barn. Sitting on a bale of hay she listened to the scratchy records, played just softly enough for the preacher to remain unaware in his bed. Her gregarious nature won her many friends at King's Garden High School, where she wore the crown of homecoming queen.

Twenty-seven years later her heart still beat to the rhythm of people. Interaction came naturally to her and, as my mom, she played an important role in my social development.

By this time in our relationship, Cyndi had noticed the size of the enormous lunch bag I brought to school — usually filled with copious slices of cheese, two peanut butter and jelly sandwiches, powdered donuts, juice drinks, and the ever-present cookie dough. She had begun to ask questions about the woman who packed these lunches and pushed me for a chance to meet her. Likewise, my mom had heard the rumors circulating and wanted to meet my "special friend." So as the Christmas season approached, I invited Cyndi to my house to join my family for our annual December 1 decorating of the tree.

Cyndi arrived that evening to find boxes brimming with tinsel and lights scattered across the living room floor. Bing Crosby's warm baritone crooned from the radio in the kitchen and the sweet scent of caramel corn was in the air.

No sooner had I greeted Cyndi at the entryway than she waltzed past me to where my mom was untangling her hands from some particularly gaudy gold tinsel. With easy grace Cyndi knelt on the floor and introduced herself, quickly joining in the task of sorting and arranging as my dad waved hello from the kitchen table. Having been forgotten in the exchange, I sat back and watched the scene unfold. I had known this girl for just a few weeks, yet I was amazed at the poise and confidence with which she held herself as she spoke and laughed with my family. She projected an image of assurance and self-worth, periodically offering a soft touch or a sincere smile. Despite the insecurities and inexperience that come with youth, her gift of valuing people flowed as naturally and beautifully as a spring creek — and my family quickly and willingly became immersed in those waters.

Cyndi seemed truly at home in my home. The lesson I learned that night was one that would echo throughout her life: She was always at home, whether she was in the steamy jungles of Indonesia or the cold halls of a hospital. Because she was always at home, she made others feel at home, too.

A few moments later my mom's younger sister, Ruth, emerged from the basement with another dusty box of Christmas decorations. Years before, Aunt Ruth had taught first graders before going to Africa as a missionary. Her vast knowledge of Scripture, complemented by her quick wit, gave her an almost biblical presence — wise and seemingly ageless. If a flannel-graph character had walked off the board into the room of my childhood Sunday school class, I would have expected her to walk and talk like Ruthie. Like so many who have remained faithful to God through unbroken years of service, she had eyes that danced with the laughter of Christ.

There was a brief moment of realization as Cyndi watched Ruthie from across the room. Cyndi then rose from the pile of tinsel and with delighted astonishment exclaimed, "You're my first grade teacher!" The unplanned reunion of Ruthie and one of her former students was underway.

The evening seemed cruelly short, and Cyndi was sent out from the house that night with hugs and smiles. With her natural sincerity, she had won over my family just as quickly as she had won over me.

I knew it was time I did something special.

∽

Herbie thought I was crazy. Though he couldn't talk, I could see in his chocolate brown eyes that he was pleading for me to find another way to express my love for Cyndi. But despite his protests, he remained at my side just as he had three years before when, as an orphan, he fol-

lowed me home from church. A comical mix of basset hound and bea-
gle, Herbie wasn't pretty but he was a survivor.

Surviving is exactly what he did that night, as I remained intent on
making Cyndi a Christmas present that was completely inspired and
unique. My plan was simple: play a few well-known songs on my guitar
and change the lyrics to revolve around Cyndi. My inability to play most
of the songs with my newly trained, guitar-playing fingers was only a
slight impediment; I was convinced that this would be a great gift.

Herbie watched as I labored in the kitchen next to the tape
recorder, repeatedly cajoling him to keep his groans to himself. Despite
my protests, Herbie continued his commentary. To emphasize his displeasure, his belly groans slid from a high to a low pitch, as if a single
tone was insufficient to communicate his displeasure. Eventually I
recorded something that was suitable for a listening audience of one.

The recording was the centerpiece of the bouquet. I needed only
to include a little "baby's breath." For this, I included three homemade
key chains I had cut from climbing rope, sewn with fishing line, and
soaked in Chap's aftershave. I jotted a quick Merry Christmas message
on parchment paper and brought it to the kitchen table where I was
assembling Cyndi's gift. I then burned the edges of the paper to give the
note an antique look — with disastrous results. I hadn't realized that
key chains soaked in aftershave might be flammable. Oh, well.
Although two key chains had perished, I figured she didn't need more
than one anyway.

Another groan from Herbie.

The next day during study hall, I slid the potently fragrant box into
the front seat of Cyndi's Jeep.

When Cyndi called that evening her voice had the lilt of happiness.
We laughed at the absurdity of many of the songs, and she remarked

that she was impressed with Herbie's harmony. She was also moved by my effort and I believed her when she said the tape had become one of her most prized possessions.

Over the next two years, Cyndi never once misplaced her keys. Smelling the way they did, they were just too easy to find.

Many teenage sweethearts become inseparable during their high school years. Somehow, Cyndi and I were able to maintain a healthy balance. We both still enjoyed the company of our friends and Cyndi's studious nature kept her grounded and focused. My life was heavily consumed by sports and the quest to play guitar like Eddie Van Halen. But most weekend nights we could be found together under the light of the moon. The hills and parks surrounding Colorado Springs afforded numerous places to dream outdoors under the stars as we shared our hopes for the future — never making bold predictions, but always hoping that we would be together.

One night in a vulnerable moment, I told Cyndi that as a boy I had been fascinated by the stars. I related how, after one particular day filled with battles between little green army men and the garden hose, my sister and I had rested beneath the crabapple tree in our front yard. Peeking through the branches and pink blossoms to the stars above, I'd felt lulled by the slow rhythm of the wind swirling the sweet fragrance in the night air. As I lay mesmerized on the late spring grass, my mind had contemplated the vast canopy of stars and I was suddenly struck by my inability to comprehend eternity in heaven. How could people live forever? What would we do in a world with no end? It was a deep and dark thought for a young boy.

When I shared this with Cyndi, I expected a reassuring hug

accompanied by a sympathetic sigh. Instead, she made a poor attempt to suppress a chuckle, then erupted into all out laughter. Cyndi being who she was, without an unkind bone in her body, somehow I felt comforted rather than put off by her playful words: "How could anyone possibly be afraid of eternity with God? It will be beautiful! Perfect! That is what we were created for! What kind of little boy were you?"

In that moment, my boyhood fear of eternity became one of Cyndi's favorite stories. For years to come, whenever I would leave with friends for a camping trip, she would yell after us, "Oh, boys, make sure he doesn't look at the stars — he gets kinda scared." Hilarious. Yet I never felt betrayed by Cyndi. Rather, her playful teasing was endearing and assured me that secrets weren't a big deal.

It was during those sweet times beneath the night skies that I began to see God's unmistakable fingerprints on Cyndi's life. She told me of how one night after youth group, she had felt distant from God. Cyndi had always attended church and had known the right answers to every question in Sunday School. But on this evening there was rejoicing in the presence of God as the angels peered over the balcony of heaven to witness Cyndi's decision to follow God not only with her mind, but also with her heart. There in the quietness of her room, she'd prayed fervently that Jesus would change her and that she would be faithful to follow Him wherever He led.

The evidence of Cyndi's conversion was powerfully evident in her love for people. She adored children, especially babies, and always was intensely joyful when with them. But Cyndi was never more moved than when she encountered people who suffered. Having spent many hours at the hospital with her father when she was a child, Cyndi was no stranger to brokenness and pain, and her heart resonated with compassion for those who were struggling. Within those sterile hospital halls, God had loved countless people through Cyndi's simple smile and attention.

Yet there were also nights when Cyndi spoke to me of her struggle with insecurity and depression. To me, it seemed a great paradox: How could she exhibit such happiness yet struggle with emotion's darker side? I didn't know how to respond, but I recognized that it was a spiritual battle through which God was leading her.

Much of our emotional bonding in those days was simply the result of young love. But in sharing our vulnerabilities we also found understanding and comfort. The burdens of adolescence were eased by the knowledge that we each had the trust and belief of the other — the intimacy shared by those who are in love.

By the end of two years filled with conversation, shared experience, and growing faith, we had nurtured a deep love and respect for one another. But the curtain of graduation loomed ahead, ready to drop and separate us. The events and decisions before us seemed overwhelming. We had no way of knowing that the hard choices we faced were just the first of many that the future held in store.

Cyndi, calling me from Westmont College.

The Ending

OF THE BEGINNING

By the grace of God, I had finally traded in my Pinto for a car four years older, but four times cooler: a 1975 Scout. One night, Cyndi and I sat next to one another in the front seat of the big four-wheel drive with much to say but no idea how to say it. Cyndi was leaving for college in California the next day and this would be our last night together.

Sitting parked just outside her house, we listened to the radio as John Denver appropriately sang "Leavin' on a Jet Plane." Afraid of making promises that would prove to be empty, we talked of the past two years and little of the future. Then it was time for her to go. She pushed the huge car door closed and, with tears in her eyes, walked toward the house. With a flair for the dramatic — undoubtedly the result of having seen too many movies — I leaped out of the car, calling her name. I ran to hug her and in doing so, realized how awkward I had made the moment. It was time to let her go.

The next morning Cyndi drove with her parents to Santa Barbara, where she would attend Westmont College. I remained in Colorado

Springs and prepared to start my senior year of high school, setting my hopes on both a state title in basketball and a new Martin acoustic guitar that I had worked for all summer. Between focusing my attention on sports and music, I somehow found time to write Cyndi almost every week. She in turn, wrote of the morning sun on the Santa Barbara hillside and of the scent of the ocean as she walked to class.

As the weeks went by, I noticed a significant change in the tone of her letters. God was moving in her life. Cyndi had begun work on Sundays with a local mission group that ministered to poor children in the community. She told me of the thrill she felt, listening to beautiful Hispanic children singing praises to Jesus while clapping in rhythm. With the help of those tiny hands, God was filling Cyndi's heart with an even greater desire to help the broken and unreached. Through those dark little eyes, Cyndi saw a world far outside of her own. God was rekindling the desire to love and encourage people that Cyndi had experienced as a little girl while visiting the hospital with her dad. A soft song was stirring and building in her heart. It was an ancient song that God had been singing all of her life, but now Cyndi was hearing the melody for the first time. God was moving her toward missions.

Twelve hundred miles away in a world forty degrees colder, my life was blissfully simple. Fall sports had ended and basketball season was beginning. Cyndi and I continued our relationship by writing and through occasional phone calls but told people that we weren't still considered a couple. We talked of seeing other people. But although opportunities arose, neither of us found in other relationships the same spirit that was in the one we had shared.

In February of 1990, my small world seemed to collapse as the mighty Colorado Springs Christian School Lions lost the district basketball championship, 102 to 98, in double overtime. I was devastated.

I'd had only three passions in high school: basketball, guitar, and Cyndi, and Cyndi was 1,200 miles away. Now, my basketball career was over.

After the game, I drove to a park overlooking the city — a place where Cyndi and I had often met. The night was cold, but as I sat on a rock looking down at the city lights, the wind and solitude were refreshing. Within, I felt a deep hurt. I had not become the celebrated basketball player I had wanted to be; I was simply average. Yet I had somehow rationalized that if I kept my chin up and played hard, the Lord would reward my efforts by giving us a state championship. That night I learned a spiritual lesson that would help shape much of my life. As He would in years to come, the Lord met me on that lonely hillside and whispered encouragement.

"I love you. I am all you need."

Late that night I called Cyndi from a pay phone. Few people knew how much basketball meant to me, but when I heard Cyndi's voice I could tell she understood. As I relayed the whole story, I once again felt the intimacy of those who have shared both dreams and loss. We were young and our dreams were small, but they were all we had and they helped bind us to one another. As we talked that night I could feel God bringing us back together, despite the physical distance between us.

After my high school graduation Cyndi returned to Colorado to join me for the summer at Woodbine Ranch, a youth camp in the foothills outside of Denver, where we both were to work as counselors. I had been accepted by Westmont College for the fall term, but Colorado had always been my home and I was reluctant to leave the mountains I loved. I believed that after an entire summer of running through the pine trees and columbine flowers, Cyndi could easily be convinced to join me at Colorado Sate University.

Cyndi loved camp. Her natural affection for children and her love of missions work came together in a virtually perfect setting. But she also struggled.

One night we had just finished singing with nearly a hundred kids around a large campfire. Easily distracted, I had been watching the brilliant orange sparks crack away from the fire, then dance and swirl into the black canopy of night. I knew the camp speaker was relaying a message of eternal significance, but the fire entranced me. Suddenly, I felt Cyndi lean heavily into my side. I looked over and her eyes were closed. My first thought was that she was sleeping. But as she slid from my shoulder onto the dirt without flinching, I knew something was wrong. We were near the back of a small outdoor amphitheater, so I was able to pick her up without attracting much attention. After struggling with her for ten minutes, I was able to bring a semi-coherent Cyndi to the nurse's station at the lodge. Cyndi spent the night there. In the morning, she was cleared to resume her role as counselor. No one could find a definitive answer as to why she collapsed. Fatigue . . . altitude . . . dehydration. In the face of so many possibilities, we went on with life as if nothing had happened.

But things continued to happen. Cyndi's energy level was dropping and her struggle with depression continued. On weekends, after the week's campers had returned home, she often felt apathetic and would cry for no apparent reason. Feeling uncharacteristically alone, she shared her experience with few people. If Cyndi felt confused by her health, I was downright baffled. I had a hard time believing that the girl who had it all together was really struggling. But behind that joyful and vivacious smile, a dark sadness lurked.

Despite those difficult times, we enjoyed our summer tremendously. In the midst of our busyness, we once again nurtured our love and respect for one another. In the pristine setting of those Colorado foothills, God was continuing His work of maturing our lives and faith. But once again, separation loomed.

~

Sitting in the back seat of my parents old brown Buick next to a box containing all of my college-bound possessions, I was headed from Colorado Springs north to Fort Collins to begin my freshman year at Colorado State. I was shocked that I had been unable to convince Cyndi to join me at CSU, but I was excited about the future. Cyndi had wrestled for weeks with the decision of whether to return to Westmont or join me. Eventually she had concluded that, at least for a semester, she would remain in California.

Walking into my dorm room on that hot August day, I found my old high school friend Mark Woody lounging on a bed in the corner. With his kind eyes, quick sense of humor, and harmonica playing skill, Mark was a perfect roommate for this new chapter in my life. Seconds later another high school friend, Ryan Christian, walked through the door. At the time, I had no clue about the significance they would later play in my life.

Ryan had been a wrestler in high school. Thin but strong, quick to laugh, and armed with a gregarious smile, Ryan was easy-going and fun. Despite his youth, he already had smile lines around his eyes from grinning so much. The three of us were a minority on that huge campus: Caucasian Christian virgins. Unfortunately, no financial aid was provided for such oddities.

After a few weeks had gone by, I felt proud that I had attended the majority of my classes. One night Mark, Ryan, and I walked past the student center lake to attend the Campus Crusade meeting that was in the biology building every Friday night. As we entered, the lights went down and music began to play. Throughout the large lecture hall, people stood to sing with the band as loud music filled the room. We stumbled our way through the dark until we found a seat near the top of the sloping auditorium. Watching the band below, I was filled with energy. All of these people, here to worship God. This was amazing!

After the meeting, I talked with a leader named Matt about music and sports. We quickly became friends, and later that week he invited me to join the worship band. God had cracked open a window and the warm breeze of opportunity was flowing in.

With Thanksgiving break coming, I couldn't wait to tell Cyndi of my college experience — and more importantly that I was playing in a band each week! As I drove her home from the airport on the first night of vacation, I chatted nonstop about the beautiful fall colors that wrapped themselves around the campus, the Walrus Ice Cream store on College Avenue, the adventures my friends and I were having, and how much I missed sharing all of these things with her. I was talking a mile a minute and probably driving considerably faster than that. During a rare break between stories, I glanced from the road to her face and saw a bemused expression I didn't quite understand.

"What?" I said. "Am I talking too much, as usual? It's just that I'm excited to see you and . . ."

She reached over, hugged me, and said, "I miss you, too."

I seized the moment.

"Cyndi, why don't you move to Colorado and go to CSU with me? The ocean is overrated. You should see this place called Verne's. They have the biggest cinnamon rolls. And — "

"I'm already accepted. I'll start after Christmas."

That January, Cyndi traded the red scooter that had carried her through the hills of Santa Barbara for a Honda Accord that performed well in snow. She enrolled at Colorado State for the winter/spring semester as an anthropology major with the intent of pursuing medical school after college. Fortunately, Cyndi was able to find an apartment close to campus and for the first time ever, we lived within a half-mile of one another.

Over the next few months, we enjoyed our time together walking through the vast fields of grass that surrounded the CSU campus and lounging by the student center pond between classes. On weekends, we took frequent drives into the nearby mountains and on a couple of occasions I coaxed Cyndi into the cool waters of the Poudre River to teach her the art of fly-fishing.

Our lives were simple, wonderful.

The following fall, I found myself eating breakfast with a long-haired man named Steve Schmutzer, a local concert promoter with Roostercrow Productions. Steve had come to hear me play guitar at Campus Crusade the previous week. As I swallowed my last bit of orange juice, Steve smiled a fatherly smile and asked if I'd like to be an opening act for an artist they were bringing to town. Having far more confidence than experience, I gave him an excited, "Yes!"

That November, I drove slowly through a snowstorm from Fort Collins, Colorado, to Laramie, Wyoming, for a fifteen-minute opening set. As I got closer, a change came over me. I was beginning to experience something that was new to me: butterflies.

Minutes before the show, I peeked through the curtain to see how many people were in attendance. It was a sparse crowd. I wasn't sure if that was good or bad. How had I ended up here, backstage, about to play songs for an audience of people? A light tap on my shoulder broke my concentration. I turned and saw a petite woman standing behind me.

"I can tell you're a little nervous," she whispered. She glanced around to make sure no one heard her comment, so as not to embarrass me. "Let's look through that curtain together."

We pulled the red velvet curtain back a few inches and peered into the semi-darkness.

"Pick one of those empty seats. Now picture Jesus sitting there with His hands in the air, clapping. He thinks you're doing great tonight!"

Although that simple action seemed a little hokey, it was an unbelievable encouragement to me that night and would continue to be for many years to come. The assurance it brought me was an echo from an earlier time:

I love you. I am all you need.

Armed with my black Martin guitar and a vast repertoire of four whole songs, I took the stage. I don't remember much from the experience other than saying the tired old line, "It's a pressure to be with you tonight," followed by the always endearing, "I'd like to inflict another song upon you." I guess we all have to start somewhere. For me that start came in a cold theater in Laramie, Wyoming. It was exactly the one I needed.

To my amazement, over the following weeks my phone rang repeatedly with more requests and invitations to play. Small churches, youth pastors, and Christian schools asked me to sing and tell my stories. I kept waiting for word to get out that I had no idea what I was doing. No one seemed to notice that was the case.

During my senior year of high school, the door to athletic greatness had closed. But as the months went by, God graciously had allowed me to follow my passion for music. Now I had to decide what to do with my remaining passion.

Cyndi.

Just married!
May 29, 1994

4

Sunrise of

OUR LIVES

SITTING AT THE NORTHEAST CORNER OF THE LIBRARY, THE HIGHEST POINT on the CSU campus, I put down my books and stared out the window at all the people below, hurriedly running from class to class. Homework wasn't really my style, so I daydreamed while next to me Cyndi studiously worked on her pre-med degree.

Still feeling a call to missions, Cyndi hoped that as a doctor she would be able to help those around the world to heal not only physically, but spiritually. As we neared graduation, her grades were outstanding and her prospects were bright. She was considering the future.

I was considering what type of mountain bike was locked to the stop sign below.

"So, where should I go to med school next year?" she asked without looking up.

It was a question I hadn't really considered. Clumsily and quickly, I changed the subject. Cyndi gave me a wry smile. She knew full well I didn't have an answer. But it was her intention to get me thinking.

And get me thinking she did. I rode my bike back to my apartment that night with much on my mind.

Two years earlier, Ryan and I had moved into an apartment off campus with his brother Chad and a friend of theirs from church, Dave Deputy. When I arrived at the apartment for the first time, I was greeted by a six-foot-five behemoth with dirty blond hair, blue eyes, and a larger than usual nose. Immediately friendly, Dave helped me carry in some boxes. Within minutes, he was leafing through my CDs. Noticing a number of Jim Croce records, Dave proceeded to tell me he was Jim Croce's long lost love child. The manner in which he delivered this joke was strangely funny, and I felt myself drawn in by his quirkiness. He then told me about sixth grade.

We had met before.

Dave had been in my class at school for one semester back in Colorado Springs. The way he recalls it, the cool kids were swinging on the monkey bars one day. As he approached to join in, looking slightly less than cool in his light green overalls, one of the kids told him there were rules to proper monkey-bar swinging. But try as he might, Dave was unable to let go with both hands while flying from one bar to the other. As a result, he was never an official member of the monkey bar club and was instead relegated to the swings, where the girls and the less manly resided.

Apparently, the rule-maker had been me.

With a history as rich as this, how could we not become best friends years later in college?

Now, in that dark and dirty apartment shared by five men and dog, Dave clasped his huge hands behind his head and leaned back in a chair that desperately wanted to give up under his weight. Looking down his great nose with a grin, Dave asked outright the question I had been avoiding: "So what are you going to do if she goes to medical school?"

Cyndi had hinted at the decision to be made; Dave had stated it clearly. It was time to cast my vote. What did I want my future relationship with Cyndi to be?

That night I lay in bed completely lost in my thoughts. I pictured Cyndi's beautiful, huge, loving smile and heard in my mind her inviting laugh. For the past six years, we had shared the trials, joys, and dreams of youth: life itself. As I lay on the top bunk with the behemoth sleeping in the one below me, I smiled into the dark. I knew what I wanted to do.

Pink clouds settled over the mountains and the spring evening seemed to come alive with excitement. It was Cyndi's twenty-third birthday and Mile High Stadium was packed with nearly 65,000 fans eager to watch the new Colorado Rockies baseball team.

One week earlier I had paid the scoreboard operator $50 to place, in the middle of the sixth inning, an important message on the Jumbotron screen that loomed high over the south stands of the stadium:

Cyndi, will you marry me? Love forever, Danny

Forty of our closest friends and family packed the bleachers. I had entrusted Ryan to hide the ring in his pocket. The only one of us who was *not* filled with incredible anticipation was Cyndi. Thinking this was all for her birthday celebration, she had no idea what was coming. She laughed and socialized the night away, looking in every direction *except* the way of the field and the huge screen.

"I need to use the bathroom," she whispered at an inopportune moment.

"You can't . . . this is a very important part of the game," I insisted. "Just wait until the inning is over, then you can go."

She gave me a quizzical look. I'd never been interested in controlling her bathroom habits before.

I tried to appear nonchalant, but I was nearly exploding with anticipation. I couldn't wait to see the reaction on her face! I watched carefully until my message finally flashed onto the scoreboard, then I nudged her side and pointed across the stadium. Her lips mouthed the words as she read the phrase, then her face erupted into a smile as she recognized what was happening. With her hands holding her cheeks she screamed joyfully and slid down into her seat, making it difficult for me to get down on one knee next to her. Ryan slipped the box into my hand at precisely the right moment and I held it out to her expectantly.

Cyndi was so excited that she forgot to say yes for nearly twenty seconds. Once she did, our group of forty began cheering, causing a commotion big enough for the entire stadium to take notice. Those shouts of joy were so loud and heartfelt that I believe in some remote part of the galaxy, they may still be ringing.

Cyndi and I planned our wedding for a year later, knowing that in order to share a future we first needed to answer some questions that God had placed in our lives. Now was the time.

I dropped out of school at Colorado State and loaded my little Subaru station wagon — the Scout's replacement — with everything I figured I would need for music ministry. Nothing but the essentials: a guitar, some clothes, beef jerky, and a sleeping bag. Having no experience with planning a "tour," I had simply made countless cold calls to college groups and churches throughout the south and up the east coast. Somehow, I had pieced together a rag-tag lineup of colleges, church concerts, and coffee house gigs for the fall.

I felt exhilarated as I drove south through Colorado, over Raton Pass, and down into Texas. This was it! I had thrown caution to the wind and placed my trust in God to literally open doors for me.

I spent the next three months playing at every conceivable venue and sleeping either in my car or on a friendly stranger's couch. It was wonderful to wake up each day in a new place with nothing but open road ahead of me and new friends in Christ behind. Every day I was learning more about God and how He had shaped me. I began to feel deep in my heart that this is what God had created me for. I wondered if God knew that I would starve if I needed to hold down a "real" job in order to make a living. Whatever the reason, God clearly was opening the door for music ministry.

I had been traveling for six weeks when I arrived at Covenant College to play for a school chapel. Upon my arrival, two good friends who attended there handed me a box of letters that had come airmail from the other side of the world.

While I was seeking answers about my future in ministry, Cyndi was thousands of miles away doing the same thing as she volunteered to work in a medical clinic in Indonesia. That day, sitting in a small dorm room on the top of Lookout Mountain, Tennessee, I was catapulted by Cyndi's writing into a world of steamy jungles that were filled with the shrill cackle of monkeys. In her simple hand she wrote of prying leaches from her skin as she trekked for miles through the vast, green backcountry to bring medicine to remote villages.

Cyndi had followed her God-given calling by signing up to serve temporarily as a medical missionary in the jungles of Indonesia. Her four-month stint allowed her to work at a clinic where local missionaries were providing medical treatment to indigenous people while sharing with them the love of Christ. Cyndi wrote of the physical beauty of the Indonesian people: their kind eyes, their brightly colored clothing, their beautiful olive skin. Despite cultural differences, she felt at home among them. This was a tremendous time of growth and understanding for Cyndi — the kind that comes only as a result of submitting completely to the Lord. In that remote world distant from Colorado in every way, God spoke to her about His plans for her life. She wrote to me:

> *Greetings from Borneo . . . Well it sounds wonderful on the road, and yes, I am ready to travel the country with you. Are you ready to travel the world with me? I must clarify this with a story. Ever since I went to Westmont, I've always wondered in the back of my mind if God wanted me to be a missionary full time. He gave me a love for people and an interest in different cultures. So I've had this little voice in the back of my head that keeps asking, "Does God want me to be a missionary?" and am I shutting Him out by not doing His will? When I decided to come to Borneo I had an ulterior motive. I wanted to see if this was where God wanted me: on the mission field. I feel at peace in my heart saying that God's answer is not now. I am so happy that God has given me such a peace about this. He has shown me what a wonderful work they are doing here but as of yet I do not feel my place is here. I would really like to do mission work for a year or two, but I don't think God is leading me . . . us . . . to full-time work here. I do feel that He is calling us to a full-time work as examples for other people around us. I've realized how much impact both you and I have on other people and I really think God is going to use us in that way. I used to think it was only you that affected other people, but God has given me*

confidence in myself and shown me that people do respond to me. I also think God has given you and me a unique way to witness for Him through our relationship. God has given us a great testimony. It makes me so happy to know that God is truly blessing and is a part of our marriage. What a team we will be for Him! I'm also excited about children. On that note, I love you.

— CYNDI

NOVEMBER 20, 1993

In the twelve months between my proposal and our wedding, we had both traveled extensively seeking God's direction and He had graciously given it. I was being called into music ministry and Cyndi was being called to support me.

May 29, 1994, was a warm and cloudless day. I stood in the foyer of Whatley Chapel in Denver, lingering for only the briefest moment before opening the door to the chapel's bridal room. Cyndi stood near the back of the room, silhouetted against brightly colored stained glass. Swirling rays of red and blue light cast an ethereal kaleidoscope of color on her white wedding dress. She had been admiring her small bouquet of roses; now she gently raised her eyes to mine as I crossed the room.

I was nearly breathless. Nothing in my life had prepared me for this moment. I searched for the perfect word or phrase that would capture what I was feeling inside but everything seemed woefully insufficient.

"You look beautiful," I told her, taking her hand.

A slow, deliberate smile rose to her lips, and the tiny tears that had been in her eyes disappeared. We prayed, thanking God for this quiet and sacred moment before the arrival of our guests.

An hour later, I stood next to my dad on the top step of the chapel as triumphant music signaled the entrance of my bride. Eager to join me, Cyndi seemed to simply float up the aisle, her escorting father merely along for the ride.

The day was hot. Very hot. The sweat began on my neck and soon made its way down my back, soaking my shirt. I turned to look at Dave and Ryan, red-faced and mirroring my discomfort in their black tuxedos. Cyndi's own expression was a mixture of joy and concentration. Sweat was dripping from her brow as she tried in vain with a small Kleenex to keep her makeup from running. Sensing my concern, she gave me a look that seemed to say, "I'm okay. Let's enjoy this!"

Halfway through the ceremony I shouldered my guitar and, facing Cyndi, sang these words I had penned the night before.

Sunrise of Our Life
When I was born my parents smiled
And held my tiny hand
As I grew they'd pray to God
For when I became a man
Loving and teaching me in all the things I'd do
For that day when I'd step forth
And give my hand to you
When you were young on your daddy's knee
He'd look into your eyes
And wonder how your mom and he
Could help to shape your life
Preparing you for that day when you would take my hand
For in the sunrise of our life

This is what God has planned

And God knew from the start

Just how to make our hearts

For what He has brought together

No man could tear apart

So here I stand before you now with my heart forever true

And here you stand before me now

Giving yours up too

Now and forever I give to you my hand

For in the sunrise of our life

This is what God has planned

WORDS AND MUSIC BY DANNY OERTLI (1994)

Despite the heat, we somehow made it through the ceremony without suffering anything more severe than minor dehydration and a great desire to feel the stirring of a breeze outside the chapel. A rented Rolls Royce waited to sweep us away, a special gift from Cyndi's parents. My arm around Cyndi's waist, we stood with our heads poking through the open sunroof, waving goodbye to our friends and relatives. The sound of joy and laughter faded in the distance as we drove into the night. Collapsing into the seat, I fumbled to find the button that would close the sunroof. Strangely, it wouldn't close. This was a Rolls Royce and the window wouldn't close? Yet it seemed fitting. The moon now had an unobstructed view of the couple it had helped bring together seven years earlier on a cold November night.

Cyndi looked tired, near exhaustion.

"Are you feeling okay?" I ventured.

"Just a little tired and hot — probably nerves and wedding stress. I'll be okay," she assured me, nearly falling asleep on my shoulder.

Our honeymoon took us to "the happiest place on earth," Disneyworld. Together, we shared an entire week filled with nothing but eating, sleeping, romance, and the occasional float through "It's a Small World."

Though our honeymoon was quiet and peaceful, after four days Cyndi was still tired. Each morning found her less rested and with new ailments. First, it was stiffness in her neck. Then sudden heat flashes, coughing fits, nausea, sore feet. . . . As the list began to add up, I worried that I had married a hypochondriac.

But again her sweet spirit persuaded me that this exhaustion was merely the culmination of planning and experiencing the biggest day of her life.

After we returned home, I reenrolled at CSU in order to finish my degree, and Cyndi began working as a receptionist at a doctor's office in town. But over the next six months, Cyndi's symptoms grew worse. She wasn't sleeping. She coughed continually. Thin to begin with, her face became gaunt and her skin seemed like a loose blanket over her bones. By this time, we knew something was very wrong; we just didn't know what. She endured test after test as she went to various doctors. To our great frustration, no one could figure out what was wrong with her.

Then the call came.

Near the end of chemotherapy, Cyndi celebrates her twenty-fourth birthday.

5

The Call

School was out, and I was enjoying a Thanksgiving break with little to do. Cyndi had traveled to Philadelphia to undergo further tests at the hospital where her father had recently taken a job. I was watching basketball on TV at my parents' house when the phone rang.

"Danny, they finally know what's wrong with me," Cyndi said. Her voice sounded tired and strangely distant. "I'm going to let you talk with my dad and he can tell you what's going on."

I was excited to finally get an answer, but something about the brevity of Cyndi's words made me wary as I waited for Larry to take the line.

"Danny, I have something very difficult to tell you but there's some good news as well. Cyndi is very sick but what she has is very treatable. She has a form of cancer called Hodgkin's disease. We'll know more later this week, but for now, it would be good if you could fly out to be with her tomorrow. I'll arrange for the flight. Danny, don't worry. She's going to be okay."

I hung up the phone in disbelief and shock, unsure of what I was feeling. My mind groped for something to hold onto, like a car needing traction to make it up an icy hill. On the other side of the room, my dad had been busily paying bills at the kitchen table. He stopped, looked over his glasses, and waited for my explanation. It was obvious something was wrong.

As I mouthed the words for the first time, reality hit me.

"Cyndi has cancer."

As I spoke, tears filled my eyes and I felt an incredible sense of heaviness and dread. The world seemed to spin faster and faster, and I felt as though a great darkness had fallen upon me.

Within hours Ryan was on my parents' doorstep; Dave and Mark quickly followed. They were as clueless as I was about how to respond, but their presence was comforting. Phone lines carried the news of Cyndi's illness across the country and an extensive prayer network developed.

As I lay awake that night, my confused mind was filled with guilt and fear. *Why didn't we discover this sooner? She's had signs that something was wrong for years. She's only twenty-three. This kind of thing only happens to older people! What if they're wrong? God, don't take her away from me, we just got married! I don't know how to take care of someone with cancer!* The questions and anxiety built through the night.

Feeling like I was moving in slow motion, I boarded the plane to Philadelphia, the gray clouds above mirroring my uncertainty. Larry picked me up from the airport and thirty minutes later we arrived at his family's home in the northern suburbs of the city.

"Cyndi is in her room," he told me. "She may be sleeping so try to be quiet."

Carefully, I opened the door to see Cyndi resting in a room decorated in white and pink. The shades were open and clouds blocked the sun as it cast its muted light into the room. Cyndi lay peacefully beneath a flowered comforter. I hesitated, unsure of how to approach her. Sensing my presence, she lifted her head and managed a weary but sincere smile. I sat beside her, stroked her hair, and gently kissed her forehead.

"At least they know what's wrong with me and can start fixing it," she said with an exhale of relief.

It was forced courage. True courage. Her resolve emboldened me. Smiling, I took her hand and, with great trepidation and fear, together we faced the future.

~

I put my music career on hold and dropped out of school once again, and we moved in with Cyndi's parents. The recommended treatment for Cyndi's cancer was eight months of chemotherapy. When we walked into Frankford Hospital, few people could have guessed that this friendly, smiling girl was on her way to her first chemotherapy appointment. Inside, however, Cyndi was anxious and frightened.

She took her seat among the mostly elderly patients in the chemo room and introduced herself to those sitting closest. Faces that at first appeared vacant and hollow soon reflected the bright, joyful life that shone from the new girl.

Less than ten feet away, beneath a protective hood of metal, the chemotherapy poisons were measured and mixed with intense accuracy. Wearing gloves, the nurse finished filling an IV bag and walked over to Cyndi to insert the needle. Cyndi pressed her head back against the recliner and closed her eyes as if the medicine were about to throw a punch. And it did. Only it took some time for the blow to be felt.

On the way home that evening we stopped for pizza. We'd been told that food would become less and less appealing to Cyndi, so we filled our stomachs with pepperoni and cheese in anticipation of the sickness to follow.

Cyndi awoke the next morning feeling better than she had anticipated. But as the days progressed, she became increasingly uncomfortable and the chemotherapy began to take its toll. Tired but jittery, hungry yet nauseous, hopeful yet fearful, Cyndi felt overwhelmed by the emotional rollercoaster.

In the weeks that followed she made a game of the inevitable hair loss. Sensing that people were uncomfortable and didn't know what to say, she did what she could to lighten the situation. As concerned people stopped to talk, Cyndi would interrupt the conversation by complaining of an itchy scalp, then with exaggerated effort she would pull great clumps of hair from her head and hold them out as if surprised by her strength.

Her hair continued to thin, and finally she knew it was time. She asked a friend to help cut the clumps of hair still on her head; then in the shower, Cyndi worked to remove the last remnants. When she emerged from the bathroom an hour later I tried my best to produce a face beaming with love and approval. But a deep sadness overtook my heart. The reality of disease that had hidden so long in her body now was evident. She now looked like a cancer patient.

The eight months of chemotherapy in Philadelphia were extremely difficult. All of our friends were still in Colorado and, despite their calls and letters, our fears about the future were compounded by isolation and loneliness.

To distract herself from the pain and nausea, Cyndi spent most days reading, sleeping, or watching old movies on TV. Having negligible skills as a cook and homemaker, I made a rather poor full-time nurse. Nevertheless, I did master the art of making Jiffy blueberry muffins. It may just have been the sight of me attempting to cook any-thing, but those muffins seemed to lift Cyndi's spirits.

Many nights she softly wept because her twitching muscles wouldn't allow her to sleep. As the fatigue and exhaustion increased, tension and frustration rose within her.

One night, we went to the drive-through at McDonald's for a quick meal. While driving, I reached over into the bag on her lap and grabbed some fries. An unfamiliar rage flashed in Cyndi's eyes and with an open hand she hit me across the mouth.

"Those are my fries!" she flared. Almost instantly, remorse over-came her and she began to cry inconsolably.

"I'm so sorry. I don't know what's wrong with me. I wish this stupid chemotherapy were done! I'd rather die than do any more treatment!"

It was a desperate plea of frustration. She was tired, sick, and scared.

After nearly eight months of chemotherapy, the doctors gave Cyndi her last treatment and her parents helped us to celebrate with a return trip to Disneyworld.

Due to her swollen feet and lack of energy, Cyndi's parents and I pushed her through the streets of the Magic Kingdom in a wheelchair, the bittersweet reminders of our honeymoon — just one year earlier — surrounding us. But despite her weakened condition, her prognosis was good and the doctors believed the cancer had been eradicated.

Sadly, two months after the completion of her chemotherapy Cyndi was once again at the hospital — this time for surgery to repair a ruptured disk in her back. The surgery was a success but her recovery would be slow, especially since her body was still reeling from the effects of cancer treatment.

We moved back to Fort Collins, feeling beaten up and tired. I enrolled in classes once again at CSU with the hope of finally finishing college and then pursuing full-time music. Cyndi planned to rest and recuperate as she again considered medical school. There in our tiny apartment, we collectively exhaled and prepared to resume a normal life together. But normalcy was not to be a guest in our home.

Christmas in Fort Collins, Colorado, 1995.

6

A Dark Fall

ONE YEAR FROM HER INITIAL DIAGNOSIS, CYNDI STILL DID NOT FEEL well. Secretly, I had begun to research cancer treatment on the Internet and was not encouraged by my findings. In most cases, cancer that returned so quickly after initial treatment was fatal. Stowing away this knowledge, I tried to remain upbeat as Cyndi continued CAT scans and other tests in Colorado to see if the chemotherapy had worked.

I was driving to the University of Colorado to perform for a Campus Crusade group on Thanksgiving night when my cell phone rang, startling me. When I reached down, I recognized the Pennsylvania area code. My heart sank. As a doctor and Cyndi's father, Larry was always the first to know of her test results, and I was sure he was calling to tell me whether her cancer had returned. In the calm and precise voice in which good doctors speak, Larry told me her latest results. Cyndi still had cancer. He asked that I tell her later that evening when I returned so that I could be with her when she learned the news.

Again, I felt sick. This time, I felt worse than I had when I first learned of her illness. And this time, I believed that she was going to die.

I hung up the phone just as I approached the CU student center. Sitting in my parked car I groaned, imagining life without her. I wanted to turn the car around and rush home to comfort her, but I was sure she had gone to bed already. We also desperately needed the money this concert would provide. I resolved to tell no one that evening and to simply get through the concert as quickly as I could.

I took the stage that night smiling but feeling the pain of death in my soul. I played for just over a minute then stopped abruptly. The crowd watched with quiet, curious faces as I sat down on the front edge of the stage. With a breaking voice, I told them that I had a lot going on in my life and that I was going to sit and play an instrumental until I regained my composure. Tears slid down the front of my black acoustic as I played a few hymns. After about ten minutes, I stood and told the audience the results of Cyndi's tests. In a moving display of solidarity, the entire group came forward, surrounded me, and prayed for Cyndi and me. The outstretched hands of those strangers represented the love and encouragement of God himself to a scared and hurting man.

Returning home late that night, I crawled into bed next to Cyndi and fell asleep with my arm around her waist, silent tears running onto my pillow.

Cyndi's next battlefield would be radiation therapy. I was surprised when her new doctor spoke optimistically about what six weeks of radiation would do to any remaining cancer. *Maybe God will spare her,* I ventured to think. Cyndi also seemed touched by this fresh optimism and approached this new treatment with less anxiety and fear.

The following week in class, I absentmindedly ran my hand inside of my shirtsleeve to scratch my shoulder. Startled, I felt a small lump protruding from the back of my shoulder. *Strange, I don't remember that being there.*

Over the next couple of days I found my hand returning to the same spot to see if it had diminished in size. It hadn't. In fact, it seemed to be growing. Reluctantly, I showed Cyndi. The following afternoon I found myself facedown on a doctor's table as he numbed my shoulder while preparing to remove what he believed was a sebaceous cyst.

"Humph."

Not exactly the sound you want to hear from a doctor who is cutting open your shoulder.

"That's not what I expected. Just to be safe, we'd better send this to the lab to make sure it's not anything serious."

One week later I listened to the clock tick as I sat in our apartment, waiting for Cyndi to come home from her radiation treatment. After she closed the door behind her, she looked quickly from left to right. The television, radio, and computer were off; there was only me, sitting at the table.

"What's going on?" she asked as she eyed me.

For the next ten minutes, I told her the news I had received that afternoon. The lump in my shoulder was cancerous. Further testing and surgery would be required to determine my prognosis and course of treatment.

It didn't take long for Cyndi to assess the situation. Having been on the receiving end of many well-intentioned words of comfort, Cyndi knew what not to do and understood what little needed to be said. She put down her bag and walked over to stand behind me. Gently, she rested my head against her chest, and I raised my hand and placed it inside of hers. We held each other in silence. Our roles had changed and in some ways, she was thankful. Now, *she* was taking care of *me*.

After more than a year of enduring dramatic medical pronouncements, we were beginning to feel somewhat jaded. So that night we dressed up and went out to Bissetti's, a wonderful Italian restaurant in the heart of Old Town Fort Collins. There, we ordered three entrees and a huge assortment of desserts. We figured, *We're both going to die anyway; we may as well die happy.* We laughed as the waiter came with the bill and I handed him my credit card, wondering if we'd be around to pay it off.

The following week, Cyndi and I had dual oncology appointments — she for her regular checkup and me for initial consultation. We entered the doctor's office at the same time and took turns sitting on the examining table. The doctor shook his head apologetically at the thought of two newlyweds having cancer. Our treatment would differ: Cyndi had already begun six weeks of radiation treatment, and I was to have surgery followed by chemotherapy.

It was a strange time. Suddenly the intensity of Cyndi's cancer was lessened by the advent of my sickness. The absurdity of the situation was almost comical and we found ourselves laughing more and worrying less — as if we were beyond the scope of normal worry, so why bother? But one unavoidable worry was money. We had none, and the bills weren't paying themselves.

I had been asked to play for a banquet recognizing the choir of a local church. At this point we were desperate, and I was happy to play for the $50 honorarium. Cyndi accompanied me, her short hair still growing back from her treatment. After enjoying a catered meal, I sang for half an hour before we packed up to leave. While we were walking through the lobby on our way out, the music minister handed me an envelope and said only that someone in the church wanted to help us. I thanked him and put the envelope in my pocket.

When we arrived home that evening, Cyndi asked about that envelope. I had almost forgotten about it. I reached into my coat and handed it to her before crossing the living room. I was hunting through the CDs when I heard an audible gasp.

"Danny, can you come over here for a minute?"

"What's goin' on?" I replied, hoping to address the issue from where I was.

A few moments went by and there was no reply so I turned my head to see if she had heard my response. Cyndi was counting. Money. I walked over to the table.

One by one, she lay a series of one hundred dollar bills on the table as she counted them out loud. Our eyes filled with tears as she ended the count at twenty: Two thousand dollars. Completely overwhelmed by the gift, we collapsed to the floor and thanked God for His goodness. Our gratitude was not just about the money. God had not forgotten us.

We never learned who had given us the generous gift.

The night before surgery to remove the tumor on my shoulder, I was again surprised by a call from Larry. He had taken the liberty of sending my test results to a specialist in Michigan to get a second opinion. Apparently, there had been a mistake because my tissue sample was not cancerous. I did not have cancer! Cyndi and I received this news with laughing thankfulness, although I was slightly concerned that my body was producing strange lumps. But at this point, who cared? What was next? What else could happen to us?

Cyndi's radiation treatment was not easy, but it was far less taxing than her chemotherapy had been. Though she often went alone, I accompanied her to as many radiation appointments as my school schedule would allow. Each time the radiation door closed behind her,

I was reminded of how serious our situation was. I couldn't even be in the same room with her as she received this intense treatment. It was a powerless feeling that left me frustrated and afraid. An invisible enemy was destroying Cyndi's life. Everything in me wanted to face it head on, fight it physically — protect Cyndi from its attacks. But there was nothing I could do.

In just over a year she had endured eight months of chemotherapy and every conceivable side effect that came with it, a back surgery, and now five weeks of radiation. How much more could her body withstand? *God please let this be the last of it,* I pleaded.

It seemed that it was. Cyndi completed her regimen of treatment and began the lengthy process of healing. She had first felt the effects of disease as a teenager; we were both now twenty-five.

That spring was one of great joy as our lives finally seemed to be getting back together. I was cancer free. Cyndi appeared to be cancer free. Walking across the platform to receive my degree in Speech Communication, I couldn't help but think of how hard the last year and a half had been. Feeling like Rocky looking for Adrian while the crowd swarmed him at the end of his fight, I quickly shook hands all the way through the line of faculty and turned to see Cyndi beaming a teary smile my way as I waved with diploma in hand.

We had survived. What could possibly happen next?

Danny, playing for a Billy Graham event.

7

Seasons

CHANGE

STIRRED BY AN EARLY SUMMER BREEZE, THE SOFT PINK BLOSSOMS OF THE crabapple tree floated to the ground in lazy circles, their sweet fragrance filling the air. As I sat on the front step of my parents' home, looking at that tree, I was surprised by how much this monument to my childhood had grown. It seemed only yesterday I had peeked through those branches into the night sky with a little boy's wonderment and optimism. Now, years later, God's gentle hands were stirring the great tree, inviting me to recapture what had been lost.

The modest, light blue house on the corner of Eagle Circle seemed the perfect place for Cyndi and me to recover and begin our lives again. Physically, emotionally, and financially bankrupt, we planned to live with my parents for six months while we got back on our feet and I began full-time music ministry.

After I'd graduated from CSU earlier that month, my dad had offered to fly me to Nashville to meet one of his college buddies who now had connections in the Christian music industry. I gratefully accepted and had arrived in Music City in May of 1995 as the stereo-

typical country bumpkin: with guitar in hand and eyes wide with inexperience. Visits to cultural meccas like Gruhn Guitars and the Ryman
Auditorium fed my senses and provided fertile ground for my dreams
to grow. Feeling somewhat more acclimated, I began a series of meet-
ings at various music labels.

For the past five years, I had traveled the country in humble style
with no regrets. But as I walked through offices covered with photo-
graphs of well-known musicians, the lure of fame was intoxicating.
Over three days, I met with numerous record producers, songwriters,
artists, and label executives. With each encounter, I became more fascinated with life in Nashville. If a record contract had been placed
before me, I would have signed it quickly.

After I'd returned to the home of my dad's friend on my last night
in Nashville, I began to get ready for bed. My eyes wandered to a gold
record that hung on the wall near where I slept. A prominent recording artist had given the record to my dad's friend in commemoration of
album sales. The shining gold surface lured me closer and I found
myself only inches away from the frame, studying the record. Slowly, my
thoughts began to crystallize and the obvious became apparent to me:
The album wasn't real gold. Before long, God had convicted my heart.

I had gone to Nashville with the intention of validating my fledg-
ling music career, to finally be recognized and rewarded. Somewhere in
my flawed thinking, I had selfishly believed that in some way God *owed*
this to me for what Cyndi and I had gone through. Then I remembered
how as a senior in high school I had sought the same recognition on the
basketball court and also had assumed God should give *that* to me.
Hadn't I learned anything? Humbled and sickened by my vain, sinful
nature, I asked the Lord's forgiveness.

Returning to Colorado, I vowed to follow God's direction and not my own path. It wasn't that I believed the record industry to be corrupt; it was my motivation that was suspect. The problem was, I didn't know what that meant for my music career. I didn't know what God wanted me to *do*.

The night I got back, Cyndi and I took a long walk. Eventually we arrived at the elementary school I had attended as a boy. While we sat on boulders just outside of my second grade classroom, I spoke of my trip and of trying to understand what God was telling me. Like many men tend to do, I quickly conveyed what I saw as the heart of the problem.

"Great story," Cyndi replied casually. "Now how 'bout some detail?"

I chuckled. She always wanted the whole story, not just highlights. I tried again, ending the story a second time with a hesitant question mark to my last sentence. I searched her eyes for approval, wondering if my storytelling this time was up to a woman's standards.

She looked away for a few moments, gathering her thoughts. "Danny, do you know why people like you?" She paused for emphasis, knowing I was a sucker for the dramatic. "Because you can't imagine that they wouldn't."

I didn't know when the car had turned, but I was pretty sure we were on a different road now. A nervous laugh escaped my lips, and I tried to decide whether or not her comments reflected well on me.

"Even now, you're coming to the conclusion that what I'm telling you is a compliment."

Darn, how does she do that?

Knowing my mind was racing to catch up to hers, she said carefully, "You have an innocence and boyish excitement that people are drawn to. Don't change what you do. Just be yourself and let God worry about the rest."

I paused, digesting what she had said. "So what I think I hear you saying is, don't worry so much. Just do my music and let God take care of everything else. Is that it?"

"Yes."

"Well, that doesn't sound so hard. Why am I making it so hard?"

"I don't know."

Suddenly, the weight of needing to prove myself was lifted from my shoulders. I no longer needed the validation of national prominence to feel my music was legitimate. I was now free to pursue music where I felt most at home: behind a microphone at some tiny church on the plains of Colorado, using just my acoustic guitar and playing songs that had little chance of ever being heard on the radio.

It was dark by the time our walk led us back to my parents' house. Strolling up Eagle Circle, I could smell the crabapple tree long before we reached the front porch steps. Not wanting this beautiful summer night to end, Cyndi and I leaned against the split-rail fence lining the driveway. After a while, she headed into the house to go to bed. I lingered, savoring the clarity that God had brought that night.

Turning toward the tree, I began to realize how much Cyndi and I had changed. For months, people had been asking what God had taught us through our experience. We had very few answers. Like a small boat tossed by the waves of a raging sea, we were simply trying to survive and reach port. We hadn't been looking for answers or explanations, just a way to stay afloat. Now that the seas were calming, we were beginning to see the beautiful damage that had been done to our ship.

Our perspective on life had been refined. The relentless waves of pain and suffering had worn away much of the pretense that had surrounded us. The excess baggage of materialism, selfish ambition, and wasted time had been washed overboard, allowing us to focus on survival. Our experience was a gift — the gift given by God to those who suffer. Suddenly, I saw suffering as God's way of removing life's nonessentials in order to reveal what is true and lasting. I realized that when life itself is threatened, people no longer care what kind of car they drive or what's on TV. Life is all that matters.

Having borne the brunt of suffering, Cyndi was well ahead of me in understanding how God uses pain. Her simple response earlier in the evening was an indication of the depth of her growth. She had exhorted me to follow the Lord by remaining in Colorado to pursue a career as an independent musician. But this wasn't the only big decision that confronted us. Cyndi was still deciding whether to pursue medical school. Hers was truly a rare mind, orderly and lightning-quick. She seemed destined for great accomplishment in life. And for so long, she had worked diligently toward the goal of medical school.

As the weeks progressed, however, Cyndi became increasingly convicted that God had other plans for her. Her interest in medicine remained, but the demanding life of a doctor became less and less appealing. She wanted a family. As a result, Cyndi made the difficult decision to forego a future in medicine in order to have children. The problem was, with all of the medical treatment her body had endured, the doctors assured us that biological children were not in our future.

But I would soon repeat Abraham's laugh at the absurdity of God's miracles. And God would soon chuckle at my lack of faith.

Cyndi and I were in for yet another surprise.

Gracie comes home from the hospital.

8

She Sees

ANGELS

OVER THE NEXT YEAR AND A HALF, CYNDI AND I DID EVERYTHING IN OUR power to enjoy life. We traveled at every opportunity. We made time for late night walks under the moon, renting old movies, and dining out at all of the quirky restaurants we'd always talked about trying. We spent much of our time with friends, playing cards and laughing until late in the evening, trying to make up for lost time.

In the midst of our renewed life together, God continued to open doors for music ministry. For the first time in my career, I had more gigs than I could handle. During the week I traveled around the region playing for various college ministries and youth groups. The weekends would usually find me playing at churches from Colorado to Wyoming and Nebraska. I also began traveling the country as a worship leader with Dare2Share: a two-day, high-energy conference designed to teach high school kids how to share their faith.

Cyndi and I began to dream of having a family. Knowing that she was unlikely to conceive, we began to look into adoption. Initially we felt disappointed that we wouldn't have a child that resembled us. Cyndi put that into perspective one day when she casually said, "At least with adoption, we'll have a greater chance of a child who can breathe normally."

"What?"

"Well, I've never wanted to say anything, but your nose is so small I wasn't sure if you were getting enough oxygen at times. With you out of the equation, we might have a child with a normal nose. That's all."

Cyndi left the room before I could respond, leaving only my little nose to comfort me. I would have cried but I wasn't sure if my tiny sniffer could take the strain.

To keep busy, Cyndi took a job at a local bank. Each day she headed out the door dressed nicely for work while I rolled out of bed into my sweats for another day of calling churches and working on music.

One morning as I was eating breakfast, I was surprised by a call from the bank.

"Um, Danny, could you please bring my water bottle? I left it at home this morning."

Immediately, I knew she was up to something. She certainly didn't need a water bottle badly enough to have me get dressed and run it down to the bank.

"Sure. I'll be there in a minute," I replied slowly, not wanting to ruin whatever surprise she had in store.

I walked in the front door of the bank to see Cyndi smiling at her desk, waiting for me. She grabbed my arm and quickly led me outside to the sunlit sidewalk.

"You must be really thirsty," I said, handing her the water bottle.

She turned the bottle over in her hands and took a deep breath. When she looked up, her mouth was fixed in a huge smile and her eyes were sparkling with tears.

"Danny, I'm pregnant."

"So, *that's* why you're so thirsty!"

"Seriously, Danny, I just took a test. I'm pregnant!"

We stood on the sidewalk looking at one another incredulously, smiling and laughing.

Over the next few months, I watched Cyndi's waistline in amazement. It seemed to grow daily. We just couldn't believe we were going to have a baby after all that we'd been through. Truly, this was a miraculous gift from God.

Four and a half months into her pregnancy, I accompanied Cyndi to her first ultrasound appointment. Filled with excitement, we watched the technician deftly work the controls of the machine as she ran what looked like a Star Trek phaser over Cyndi's exposed abdomen. Black and white images appeared on the monitor and I leaned forward, hoping to see the form of a baby. Unfortunately, all I saw was what looked like a kidney bean and the word "yolk sac."

"Can you tell if it's a boy or girl?" I ventured.

The technician furrowed her brow.

"Well," she said. "It's a very hairy baby."

With all of the chemo that Cyndi had received, my first thought was that we were going to have Bigfoot Baby, perhaps a new breed of superhero. Having read many comic books as a kid, it seemed feasible. Maybe my child would have super powers like Spider-Man or the Incredible Hulk.

I asked again if the baby was a boy or girl. For the next thirty minutes, the technician did everything in her power to solve the riddle. But we left the office knowing only that our baby had a full head of hair that was detectable even by ultrasound — and that he or she liked to keep his or her legs crossed.

Although we did not discover the gender of the baby, the ultrasound was an extremely moving experience. In an intimate moment with the Lord, I wrote this song:

Four and 1/2 Months

I don't know the color of your eyes

Or the color of your hair

But I see you just the same

I don't know the sound of your laugh

Or the sound of your cry

But I hear you call my name

And I don't know what you'll be wearing

And I don't know if it's pink or it's blue

How could I love you any more

You are the precious answer to what I've prayed for

And in my heart of one thing I'm sure

How could I love you any more

I don't know if your nose is mine

Or if your chin is hers

But I know we're each a part

I don't know the touch of your skin

Or the touch of your hand

But I feel you in my heart

And I don't know when you'll say daddy

And I don't know when you'll stand on your own

(chorus)

WORDS AND MUSIC BY DANNY OERTLI (AUGUST, 1997)

Four months later, just as we were getting ready for bed, Cyndi's water broke. We raced to the hospital. There wasn't a dire emergency, as Cyndi's labor was moving forward reasonably slowly; I just had always wanted to tell a police officer after I'd been pulled over for speeding, "Quick, turn on your lights and lead us to the hospital. We're having a baby!" Unfortunately, that didn't happen and we arrived at the hospital quietly and without fanfare.

Cyndi's labor progressed over the next twenty-four hours. Then the moment finally arrived. She gripped my hand with a strength I didn't know she possessed while she focused on her breathing. The minutes ticked by and then a tiny head slowly came into view. After a few moments of struggling with it, the doctor delivered our baby. He gently cupped his hands beneath the tiny form and carefully presented to Cyndi and me a beautiful baby girl. A thousand silent prayers surged through my body as I marveled at the miracle of life. I was overwhelmed with joy. The presence of God saturated the room; it was as if the very air we were breathing were infused with His pleasure and joy.

As we were inhaling the beauty of the moment, the doctor ordered everyone from the room. Within seconds, a nurse wrapped the baby in a blanket and handed her to me, motioning for me to follow her. Dazed, I asked what was happening but received no reply. I leaned over and kissed Cyndi on the forehead before leaving the room, assuming I'd return quickly. Over my shoulder, I could hear the urgency in the doctor's voice as he tersely said to the remaining nurses, "blood — stat."

"She'll be fine. They just need to stop some bleeding," the nurse assured me. "Let's get this little baby cleaned up!"

I sensed something was wrong and I paused, wondering if I should go back to the room and stay with Cyndi. But the hospital staff seemed to have everything under control and the little bundle in my arms allayed my fears. I followed the nurse to a small washbasin. With skilled hands, she laid the tiny baby down on a counter and peeled back the folds of the blanket to reveal tiny fingers and toes, stretching out into their new world. For the first time, I was able to study every feature on this little child. My child. The name Cyndi and I had chosen fell through my smiling lips as I said over and over, "Gracie. Gracie."

"Grace. Hi, I know my voice may sound a little different to you now, but I'm your daddy. Remember, the one who played guitar next to mommy's tummy? It's me! Do you recognize my voice?"

The nurse gave me a knowing smile, most likely having witnessed hundreds of similar interactions. After awhile, she turned to me and with playful exaggeration said, "This baby has more hair than any baby I've ever seen!"

I looked down and realized that she had been washing Gracie's hair for quite some time. I thought back to the moment she had been delivered. I remembered noticing some hair. But as the nurse cleaned her up, it seemed as if a lion's mane was growing out of her little head. By now my mom had joined us and we all laughed incredulously as baby Gracie was dried off and placed back in her blanket with a huge pillow of hair to rest on.

Just then, the doctor approached me.

"There's been some hemorrhaging and we've taken Cyndi to surgery to stop it," he said.

My heart sank. Even though I wouldn't have been able to do anything, I felt guilty for having left her. *Why hadn't I stayed by her side?* I was angry with myself and distressed that she was facing this alone.

The doctor and I spoke for a few more moments, then I took my seat in the waiting room. Mark Woody, my old friend and college roommate, came by to help me pass the time. With great care, he helped to ease my mind as we shared stories and reminisced about old friends. Gracie was sleeping in the room next door with a handful of other newborn babies. But for some reason, I didn't want to be with her until I knew that Cyndi was okay.

After an hour, the doctor found me in the waiting room, nearly passed out from exhaustion. He informed me that everything had gone well and that Cyndi would soon be moved to a room where she could recover.

That night, I slipped into Cyndi's room and fell asleep on a chair by her bed. I awoke to the slightest stirring of movement. The room seemed a misty gray as the predawn light crept through the blinds. I looked over at Cyndi but her heavy breathing assured me she was in a deep sleep. Again I heard a noise and turned toward the door as it quietly opened, light from the hallway spilling into the room. Shielding my eyes from the brightness, I could just make out the silhouette of a dark form quietly padding into the room, pushing a cart. I sat up. There before me on the cart lay a tiny bundle of blankets, on top of what looked like a clear basin. The nurse put her finger to her lips and quietly placed the cart next to Cyndi and me. Before I knew it, she had slipped away.

Peering over the top, I could see Gracie sleeping peacefully. I reached out to touch her face. She was warm, serene. Then I heard Cyndi rustling behind me.

"Can you bring her to me?" she said in a tired voice.

With exaggerated care, I picked up Gracie and placed her next to her mother.

Cyndi shifted position and lay on her side to get a better view. Gently, she peeled away part of the blanket covering Gracie's face. As she stroked Grace's cheek, Cyndi kept repeating, "I love you so much. I love you so much."

It wasn't so much her words that were memorable on that early morning; it was the soft intensity of her eyes. Watching the two of them, I couldn't help but feel their souls were soaring in a spiritual dance, the deep love and laughter of the Creator resonating in their hearts. This was the pinnacle of human emotion, as close to the joy of heaven as mortal bodies can get.

～

Gracie's hair was an accurate indicator of her personality: wild. An abundantly active and charismatic child, Gracie consistently drew attention with both her mane of wavy brown hair and her loud squeals. But one of her most distinctive activities happened at night. Gracie entertained visitors.

Before she could stand Gracie would sit for hours at a time in her crib, looking up at the dark ceiling, waving and babbling in apparent conversation.

One brisk fall night, as the leaves blew through the neighborhood like little tornadoes, Cyndi approached me while I was sitting on the couch, relaxing.

"You need to see Gracie."

I followed her up the stairs to Gracie's room. Taking care not to be seen, we tiptoed through the doorway. The moon bathed the room in silver light and the sound of Gracie's babbling filled the air. The word *Graceland* seemed to glow on the wall near her crib where a friend had hand-painted it in white.

Gracie's head flopped from side to side as she spoke nonsense to the ceiling. Reaching her chubby hands into the night, she appeared to be grasping at something.

Cyndi cupped her hand to my ear and whispered, "I think she sees angels."

That night I lingered at my office window after everyone had fallen asleep. Looking down at the backyard, the leaves still whirling through the air, I was inspired. I stayed up until morning light and penned this song:

She Sees Angels

I've seen this before so I turned out the light

And walked across the room

The wind played its song through the trees in the yard

The shadows were chased by the moon

I stood in the doorway and let out a sigh

And watched the small little girl

Who was there in the moonlight sitting up in her bed

Tossing her head in a whirl

And she sees angels

Dancing in the sky

She sees angels

In the night

Do they whisper sweet words, do they sing her a song

Do they light up her eyes with the stars

Do they touch her soft skin as she sleeps late at night

Does she even know who they are

Floating in air they perform their ballet

Lifting their praise to above

For sweet little girls bathed in heavenly light

Learning the ways of God's love

(chorus)

WORDS AND MUSIC BY DANNY OERTLI (OCTOBER, 1998)

We did not know that God would call upon those angels to minister to Gracie in the very near future.

God was moving.

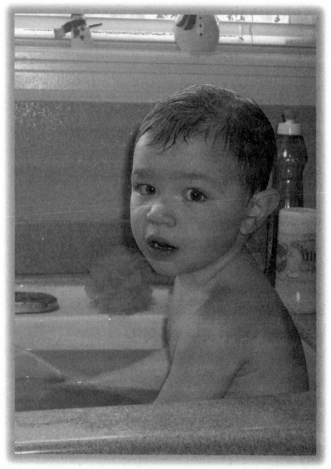

Jack enjoys a bath in the kitchen sink.

9

A Late

NIGHT PRAYER

As Gracie grew, so did Cyndi's desire to have another child. Physically, her body had come a long way. She was regaining strength and stamina, and the fear that her cancer would return diminished with each passing season. Her depression had abated as well and for the first time in many years, she was beginning to feel healthy not only physically but emotionally.

But once again, the severity of her cancer treatment caused complications. Cyndi was experiencing symptoms typical of early menopause. After yet another series of tests, the doctors assured us that despite our little hairy miracle, it was extremely unlikely that we would have a biological child again.

Any sense of loss that we felt at not being able to have another biological child was quickly replaced by eager anticipation. We had always wanted to adopt. The prospect of God bringing us a child in need for us to love was invigorating. We both felt there was no greater way we could serve God.

We searched through the file cabinet until we found the folder labeled "adoption" that we had compiled before Gracie was born. Laying it on the table, we leafed through various brochures and prayed that God would lead us down the right avenue.

After a few days of researching various organizations and talking with friends who had adopted, we believed that God was directing us to a smaller agency located near our home in Denver. It was a Christian ministry that placed a high importance on the care of the birth mom. The agency seemed a great fit for us and we methodically worked our way through the legal paperwork. We were also faced with questions that forced us to reconsider our values and objectives in life. *Would we consider a baby of mixed race? Would we adopt an older child? Would the presence of any physical or mental deficiencies cause us to terminate the adoption process?*

With Cyndi's complicated medical history, we weren't sure how to answer many of these difficult questions. Many of the proposed scenarios seemed exceedingly difficult if she were to have any further physical limitations. However, God continued to grant us peace with our decision to adopt and we were certain He had called us to serve Him in this way.

Cyndi was more excited than I had seen her in years. The thought that some young mother might be carrying a baby for us in her womb at that very moment was almost more excitement than she could take. Many times we'd be walking in the mall and Cyndi would nudge my side and raise her eyebrows as a pregnant woman walked by. To her, every baby was potentially her baby.

After completing the paperwork, we braced ourselves for the emotionally draining process of waiting for a birth mom. Unbelievably, the phone rang one month later.

"Hi, Danny, this is Pam at Christian Family Services. Well, you're not going to believe it, but we have a birth mom that would like to meet with you tomorrow."

After talking for a few more moments I hung up the phone, my mouth open in disbelief and excitement.

"Cyndi, could you come up here for a minute," I yelled downstairs.

As she entered the room she eyed me cautiously, although I had tried to sound casual. I wondered, *How does she always know when something is up?* "That was the adoption agency." I paused, eager to watch her excitement boil over. "They have a birth mom who wants to meet with us tomorrow afternoon."

Cyndi covered her mouth with her hand and gasped.

"Now, they didn't say anything about her nose. Would you like me to ask them if it's bigger than mine before I confirm our appointment?"

Cyndi politely acknowledged my joke with two short chuckles, but it was clear that her mind was racing ahead to the meeting.

When I awoke the next morning, Cyndi's wide eyes were only inches from my face.

"What are you doing? You're creeping me out."

"I'm just so excited. I couldn't sleep."

"All night?"

"Yeah, pretty much!"

The morning passed painfully slowly until it was finally time to drive to the agency.

When we got inside, we saw a young girl seated on a couch between her parents. Unable to help herself, Cyndi crossed the room in a few strides, reached down, and gave the girl a hug. I remained in place, muscles tensed, ready to reciprocate a hug if it came to that but not comfortable enough to initiate one.

After official introductions were made, we all settled into our seats for the meeting. Cyndi and I were asked to share the story of how we met and where life had taken us since. Cyndi's voice quivered with emotion as she described the events of the last few years. I could sense Cyndi's insecurity as she did her best to reassure a birth mom who might be reluctant to give her baby to a woman who had recently had cancer.

We left the meeting knowing we hadn't answered every question with practiced skill, but feeling that a positive connection had been made.

A week later, Pam from the adoption agency called and informed us that we had indeed been chosen to raise this young girl's child. Cyndi was overjoyed. That entire evening, she was unable to wipe the smile from her face. Holding Gracie's little hands, she sang little songs about the new baby coming into our home and all the fun the two of them would have. Gracie returned her smile with wide eyes having no idea what was about to take place.

The baby was due in early August. Cyndi kept busy during the five months of waiting by cleaning and reorganizing most of the house. She also loved to sit on the couch and look at the baby clothes in all the mail-order catalogs, dog-earing each page she wanted to remember when the baby was born. I began to write songs and plan for a new record that I hoped to release by the end of the year.

On August 13, 2000, I was scheduled to play for our home church in Parker, a southern suburb of Denver where we had been living since my college graduation. After leading worship for the first service, I slipped out the side door as the pastor began praying before his sermon. Cyndi greeted me with a chocolate covered donut resting on her open palm. I took the donut, she took my arm, and we made our way around the corner to the long hallway that led to the front foyer. There, Cyndi abruptly stopped. Following her gaze, I looked down the hallway to see

Pam smiling and waving in our direction. *What is she doing here? She doesn't go to church here. Wait a minute . . .*

We walked briskly toward one another and met midway down the hall.

"It looks like there might be a baby born today," Pam said with great delight.

Cyndi had been preparing for this moment for months. She raced home in her minivan to grab the bag she had packed with clothes, reading material, toiletries, and a camera. She was ready for a long stay at the hospital.

That afternoon, we did our best to remain patient as we watched and listened to the clock on the hospital wall, marking the passing hours. I had a concert scheduled for that evening and Cyndi urged me to go. She reminded me that labor is a long process and that I should go ahead and fulfill my commitment. "You won't miss anything," she assured me.

She lied.

Just as I was pulling up to the church for sound check, my cell phone rang.

"Danny, you have a son!" Her voice was alive with happiness but her continual sniffing told me how emotional this had all been. She had desperately wanted to be in on the labor but wasn't sure if the birth mom's family would want to keep that moment private. My concern for her emotions was relieved at her next statement.

"It was beautiful!" she said, holding out the "u" in beautiful.

"What? I thought you said her labor was going to take awhile. I missed it? I'm turning around right now!"

"I know, I'm sorry. It happened really fast. But, since you've already missed the birth, just do your concert and then get up here."

It was the shortest concert of my career. Completely distracted, I flew through a quick set of songs and jumped in my car to meet my new baby boy.

Cyndi was in the lobby when I arrived and she led me upstairs to where my son was waiting. There had been some unexpected complications with his heart and, as a result, he was hooked up to various pieces of medical equipment.

"Isn't he beautiful?" she said lovingly, touching his head. "Do you still like the name Jack? I think that's what we should name him."

"Jack it is. I love that name," I assured her.

Over the next few days Jack was kept in the hospital for observation. There had been some abnormality with his heart rhythms, and the doctors wanted to be sure he was stable before we took him home. Added to that, Jack's birth mom didn't want to leave until she knew he was okay. As a result, she spent much of her time holding baby Jack. It was a difficult time for everyone.

Cyndi especially struggled. She knew this young girl was giving us the ultimate gift and that she had every right to hold and love the baby she had helped to create. But we had heard of many cases in which the birth mom became attached and then changed her mind about relinquishing the baby for adoption.

After a few days, the doctors assured us that Jack was healthy enough to leave. Continuing her nesting phase, Cyndi actually had the car cleaned and detailed for Jack's ride home.

Jack quickly fell asleep as we gathered around his brand-new car seat in the lobby of the hospital. Pam eloquently asked God's blessing on this young boy's life. Anxious to take Jack home but hesitant to appear too eager, we lingered for a few more moments with Jack's birth mom and her family. The bittersweet exchange culminated in one final hug good-bye.

As we walked out to the car, Cyndi's face reflected the conflicting emotions we were feeling. We were unbelievably thrilled that we would be able to love and raise this baby. At the same time, our hearts broke for the young girl still standing in the lobby, watching her precious child being taken home to another family.

Somehow Cyndi made it all the way home without getting carsick, despite the fact that she faced backward, talking to Jack, the entire trip. I'm pretty sure he was asleep, or at least pretending to be, but that didn't seem to slow her down any.

At home, I set Jack's car seat on the kitchen table like a sack of groceries and wondered when three-year-old Gracie would notice her new baby brother. With sincere joy, she pulled up a chair next to Jack and began telling him everything about herself and emphasizing it was okay to be adopted.

Meticulously and lovingly, God had woven Cyndi's, Gracie's, Jack's and my stories together, making from our lives an ornate and diverse tapestry. Both children had come to us through such unique circumstances, it was obvious God had a specific purpose in creating our little family.

Late one night when I was putting Jack to bed, it occurred to me that the times of greatest growth in my life always had been times of intense difficulty and suffering. As I looked down at Jack's tiny form in the moonlight, it pained me to think that he too would suffer someday. I wanted to hold him, shield him from the evil in the world and protect him from any harm. Those thoughts quickly evaporated as God reminded me in my spirit that He loved this child even more than I did.

I wanted a godly son. And if what the Bible says is true, fire brings refined gold. I stayed up that evening, meditating on the relationship between those two truths as I wrote this song for Jack:

I Thought You Should Know

It started on the day you were born

I wanted you to have everything

But now it seems my conscience is torn

Between what I desire and what I believe

What kind of man would I be

If I didn't pray for you

What my father prayed for me

So I pray with all my heart

That you would be broken

And in brokenness find God

And I pray that you will fall

And in falling down you'll stand up

To rise above it all

I pray that God would break you as you grow

I thought you should know

As you walk down your winding road

Faith and hope will go a long way

And you'll learn all you need to know

That life is hard but love remains

I wish you nothing but the best

So I'm asking God

To put you to the test

(chorus)

WORDS AND MUSIC BY DANNY OERTLI (AUGUST, 2001)

I could not have known that this prayer would be prophetic.

Danny and Cyndi
Christmas, 2001

10

God's Hand

IN THE WAVES

SEVEN DRAMATICALLY DIFFICULT AND EVENTFUL YEARS HAD PASSED SINCE Cyndi and I stood at the altar and promised to love one another, no matter what came our way. In that time, our love for one another had deepened tenfold. The carefree and whimsical spirit that characterized our early love had been replaced by a deep commitment and understanding of what love truly is: standing hand-in-hand while facing life's greatest battles.

As time passed, our lives finally began to resemble some sort of normalcy. Cyndi's depression still surfaced on occasion, but for the most part, emotionally she was solid. She also had begun to regain physical strength through steady exercise and healthy nutrition and for the first time in quite a while was feeling healthy.

By God's grace, we had become parents. Who would have believed on the night of Cyndi's initial cancer diagnosis that one day we would have two children? Every time I flew home from a concert to meet Cyndi and the kids at the airport I was again reminded of God's compassion and mercy. We were a family!

Gracie had proven to be a handful in those early years. Many times, Cyndi and I wondered if her wild antics and supreme confidence were a result of something we had done wrong in her upbringing. But God continued to assure us that Gracie's spunk, if channeled properly, would someday take her even further than we could imagine.

At the same time, Jack was quite possibly the easiest child ever born. Mellow and sweet, he was usually content to stay in one place and rarely found himself in trouble — Gracie found enough for both of them! Cyndi loved Jack, just as she loved Gracie. Her days revolved around holding him and it always brought a smile to my face to see them cuddling together. Cyndi had always wanted to be a mom. This was her time. At last, she was in her element.

I was beginning to feel that we may have finally put sickness and disease behind us. I wanted so badly to soak up all of the beautiful moments happening around our home that I often found myself watching almost as a detached observer. After such a long road, it all seemed too good to be true. Cyndi, my high school sweetheart, had survived. We had two beautiful children. Life was sweet.

~

People walking by could not have guessed that some of the best musicians in the world were gathered behind the plain, businesslike front of the building that housed Total Access Studios in Redondo Beach, California. I opened the door and heard music coming from the next room. Turning the corner, I saw Pete Nelson — guitarist for The Kry — hunched over a song chart making changes with a pen. He looked up to greet me with a smile.

Pete was the brother of a good friend, and I had long admired his guitar playing from a distance. Eventually, our paths crossed and Pete and I had become friends. After years on the road, Pete was now a pastor in Denver. With a sharp mind and a love for people, Pete excelled as a leader and shepherd. But, true to his first ministry love, he still retained connections within the music world.

With great expectations, I had asked Pete to produce my new record three months earlier. Sitting in his church office that day, I'd watched in amazement as he thumbed through the phone numbers of the players he wanted to enlist for the project. One by one, Pete had assembled an all-star cast of some of the finest musicians around. Now that production had finally begun, I stood at the entrance to the studio feeling a mixture of intimidation and giddiness. Taking a deep breath, I opened the door and we began production on *Nothing Left to Prove.*

Four months and thousands of dollars later, Christmas 2001 saw the near completion of that enormous undertaking. Cyndi and I had invested virtually everything we had in the project and were excited that in one month's time the record would be released.

To celebrate the completion of the album, and as a gift to a hard-working young mom who didn't get nearly enough romance in her life, I snuck into the basement on Christmas Eve to prepare a special present. Carefully, I placed a new black evening dress in a box and lay a typewritten note on top before wrapping it. The note read:

> *Cyndi,*
>   *You'll need this dress for a very special occasion . . .*
> *Just for you for Christmas . . .*
> *4 days in Hawaii.*
>
>   *Love, Danny*

Cyndi was ecstatic. Immediately, she began to plan for the trip. She looked up our hotel on the Internet to see what type of clothes she needed to bring and researched the island to see what type of excursions were available — snorkeling, helicopter tours, hiking, and shopping being some of her favorite options.

Not a day went by that she didn't give me a hug or a kiss to thank me for our upcoming getaway. If this was her response, I figured, I should have done this much earlier!

We counted the days until our vacation and Cyndi went to a local tanning booth to prep for the trip. When the day finally arrived, however, Cyndi was strangely hesitant. After checking our bags with the ticket agent, she pulled me aside.

"Danny, are you sure the kids will be okay? I have a strange feeling about this."

She actually began to tear up and I could tell she was serious.

"Cyndi, you need this. Besides, your mom is here to take care of them. They'll love that. Besides . . ." I distracted her with brochures from our hotel.

That afternoon, Cyndi and I held hands and anxiously peered out the airplane window as mile after mile of deep blue ocean stretched beneath us on our way to the Garden Island, Kauai.

Later in the evening we stood on the balcony of our hotel room as tiki torches swept an orange glow through the courtyard. The night was magical. In the distance, dark waves surged until they were ripe with foam, crashing into the rocks lining the shoreline. We stood in rare silence, enjoying the tranquility and majesty of the moment, inhaling the grace and mercy in our lives that seemed to be carried on the night air.

The following days were filled with beauty and adventure as we explored the island. The lush green rain forests of the island's interior sloped down to meet magnificent white beaches. In every direction, the turquoise-green Pacific stretched into the distance. From one lookout, it seemed as if we could almost make out the great fingers of God, reaching down into the water and flipping the waves toward the shore. Mile after mile, our senses were filled with evidence of the Creator's grandeur and playfulness.

On our second to last afternoon, we drove inland toward the Grand Canyon of the Pacific: Waimea Canyon, in Kokee State Park. We left the car and hiked a short distance to an observation point overlooking the valley. A light haze settled across the vast canyons as shades of deep red and purple painted the chasm walls.

As I reached down to open the camera bag, I noticed Cyndi leaning heavily against the rail, looking pale and out of breath.

"Are you okay?"

"Yeah, I think I'm just out of shape. That's pretty sad. That wasn't even a very big hill!" Neither of us suspected anything of significance had happened and we continued on. With the beautiful canyon as our backdrop, we stood arm-in-arm while a fellow tourist snapped our picture.

That short hike set in motion events that had been ordained before the beginning of time.

When we returned to our hotel a few hours later, Cyndi complained of dizziness and shortness of breath. She lay down and quickly fell asleep.

The next morning, I awoke to an ocean breeze and an empty bed. The balcony door was open and the wind was lightly blowing the drapes in and out of the room. I rose and walked to the balcony, expecting to see Cyndi there. But she was gone. Nearly half an hour later, she opened the hotel room door. She was wearing a sweatshirt and shorts and carrying a towel and her Bible.

"Where'd you go?"

"Well, I couldn't sleep so I thought I'd watch the sunrise from the beach and have a quiet time. It was absolutely gorgeous! I wanted to come back and wake you up but you seemed to be sleeping pretty hard. It was wonderful!"

Later, I would wonder what that conversation must have been like. What did the heavenly Father whisper to his daughter in that sacred moment on the beach? Was it a whisper of His love for her on the wind? Did she marvel at His power and majesty as the waves thundered around her? Did the early morning sun rising over the ocean speak to her soul, reminding her of God's immensity, His faithfulness? A night's rest had helped Cyndi to feel better, but I could tell that she was still struggling. As I watched her pack with vacant eyes and listless hands, I fought the urge to be angry. *Why is she always sick? Can't we just enjoy a vacation without her coming down with something? Lord, don't You think we've had enough?* I was tired of Cyndi being sick and she was even more tired of being sick. The undercurrent of a spiritual battle began to create a tension between us.

After we left the hotel, we drove to the Calvary Chapel of Kauai, where I was to play that morning. We walked through the door and our spirits lifted as we were greeted with warm smiles and Hawaiian leis. It was one of the friendliest churches I had ever played for. One by one, church members engaged us in conversation and asked how they could serve us. It became difficult to continue our petty argument in this environment. From across the room we caught each other's eye and exchanged a look that meant both *I'm sorry* and *I love you.* I was the more sorry of the two; at least she had an excuse.

As I was doing the sound check, a man with a camera asked Cyndi to join me on stage for a quick picture. She jumped onto the platform and threw her arm around my shoulder, eager to get back to her seat. It would be the last photograph ever taken of Cyndi.

That night after the concert, we flew from Honolulu to Denver. Whatever medical difficulties were affecting Cyndi, we decided, could wait until we got home. We landed in Denver at seven AM. The day was Monday, February 4, 2002. While we waited for my dad to pick us up, I turned to Cyndi and apologized again for my attitude toward her. She put an arm around me and said, "It's okay. I just want to go home and see the kids."

Despite not feeling well on the drive home, Cyndi could hardly wait for the car to come to a stop when we got there. Quickly she leaped out of the vehicle; Grace and Jack were there to greet her. Taking both kids in her arms, Cyndi nearly hugged the breath out of them. She reached into her bag and pulled out a Hawaiian doll for Gracie. Gracie's eyes sparkled as she began stroking the doll's long black hair. Jack looked on, completely unaware that he was to get a present as well. When Cyndi placed the beaded necklace around his neck, his little face lit up with surprise at the simple gift — a complimentary token from the hotel.

After about fifteen minutes spent solely with the kids, Cyndi said her good-byes to all of us in the kitchen.

"I love you, Jackie!" she said as she leaned down to kiss his forehead.

"And Gracie, I can't believe how big you got since I left! What a big girl!"

Gracie was obviously pleased by this comment and Cyndi bent down and gave her a big squeeze followed by a kiss. Turning to me, she gave me a quick, gentle peck on the cheek.

"I'll be back soon." Then she was out the door with her mom to go to the doctor's office. On the flight home we had decided that her shortness of breath was probably a result of lingering radiation effects and nothing serious to worry about.

Thirty minutes later, however, the phone rang. Cyndi's mom sounded distracted and out of breath.

"Cyndi collapsed while signing in at the doctor's office and they're trying to resuscitate her. I'll call you back when I know more."

Feeling shocked but strangely calm, I asked the kids to join me on the living room floor. I was careful not to frighten them as I prayed, asking that God would take care of mommy and that she would feel better.

The phone rang again as I said, "Amen."

"Hi, Danny? I'm the receptionist here at the doctor's office. They've taken Cyndi by ambulance to the hospital. You need to meet her there. I don't know any more than that."

My dad had left earlier so I was alone with the children. I made a quick call. Within moments, a neighbor came to watch the kids and I jumped into the car to head to the hospital. While I was still halfway there, God began to prepare my heart. I had an overwhelming sense that Cyndi's life might be ending. It wasn't a feeling of despair, just the realization that this crisis was different than the other things we had gone through. I remember feeling a supernatural peace as I prayed, *God, You love her more than I do. Your will be done.*

I arrived at the hospital just as my mom and Cyndi's brother Grant were parking their cars. The three of us hurried into the emergency room and I asked the security guard where I could find Cyndi Oertli. With a worried look he asked us to wait, then turned and walked through double doors. A few minutes later, a hospital counselor appeared and led us down a different hall, into a waiting room.

By now, I knew that something had gone drastically wrong.

Looking weary and drained, Cyndi's mom opened the door and joined us as we waited for the doctor. She knew little more than we did. Seconds later, the door opened to a man in hospital scrubs with sweat on his brow. He asked which of us was Cyndi's husband. I raised my hand and he carefully situated himself directly in front of me. Resting his forearms on his knees, he leaned forward and began to speak. His voice was distant as I watched his lips move up and down. I remember noticing his nonverbal communication: direct eye contact, a touch of the hand every so often, the steady cadence of his words. Knowing he was trying to comfort me, my mind leaped ahead to the obvious conclusion. After nearly a minute, I broke out of my fog to hear him say, "We did everything we could."

He then motioned to the door behind me and asked if I'd like to say good-bye.

My first thought was, *What am I going to say to the kids? How can I tell them?* I asked Grant and Ruth if they'd like to see her first. They walked through the door and I rose to leave the room, as if walking away would somehow change the circumstances. I stumbled down the hallway, conscious of people's stares. Near the end of the hallway, I saw my brother-in-law, Andy, as well as my dad and sister, talking to an attendant. I tried to raise my voice but was unable to speak. With a great force of effort, I cried out, "Susie!" and fell over at the waist from the exertion.

They rushed forward and helped me up. I told them that Cyndi had died and pointed in the direction of the room we had gathered. Still wanting to put distance between me and what was happening, I asked them to go in and I walked outside.

Standing on the curb, I made a desperate cell phone call to my close friend and roommate on the road, Greg Stier. The energetic president of Dare2Share, Greg had become one of my closest friends during our time traveling together. In broken sentences, I told him what had happened. Greg promised that he would be there soon. I didn't know he was in Florida at the time.

I remained on the curb for another ten minutes, my mind reeling with pain and confusion. I wanted to rush into the hospital, to find Cyndi and *will* her back to life. I wanted at least to have been there to hold her as she died. *How could I have left her alone? No one knew her as I did. No one!* Had she been frightened? I couldn't bear the thought of her scared and alone as she took her last breath. She was my bride. My closest friend. The mother of my children. I couldn't imagine life without her. *After all that we have been through, how could it have ended this way?* The total sense of loss was deeper and more cutting than I ever could have imagined.

Gathering my waning strength, I shuffled back to where the family had gathered in the same room where the doctor gave us the news. Wordlessly, I made my way past them into the adjoining room where Cyndi had been taken.

The door clicked closed behind me and then there was complete silence. Cyndi lay on the table with a sheet pulled up nearly to her chin to cover the trauma and bruising her body had received as doctors had worked to revive her.

She was completely still. No movement. No breathing. For a moment, we seemed suspended in time. Knowing it was foolish to do so, but unable to resist, I put my ear to her lips to listen for any sign of breathing. As the seconds ticked by, the finality of Cyndi's death hit me. With a heave of my shoulders, I fell to my knees beside her and let out a groan of pain and grief.

"Cyndi, I'm so sorry. I'm so sorry." The words slipped from my lips.

Remembering what an old friend had told me about his actions following his dad's death, I placed my fingertips on Cyndi's eyelids and prayed, "Thank you, Father, for these eyes that saw the world and recognized your beauty."

Taking her hand in mine, I whispered, "Thank you, Father, for these hands that worked diligently to mold and shape the lives of my children."

Finally, with great effort, I placed my hands on her heart, "Thank you, Jesus, for this heart that beat for You."

Then I left the hospital and my dad drove me home to Gracie and Jack.

Cyndi and I, just before I played at Calvary Chapel of Kauai.

11

All the

SCATTERED PIECES

MY DAD PULLED INTO MY DRIVEWAY AND OPENED THE PASSENGER DOOR before I even knew he had gotten out of the car. He held my arm and walked beside me as we hobbled up the walk. Next to the door handle was a hand-painted plaque Cyndi had bought during our first year of marriage that read "*The Oertlis.*" I eyed the brightly colored flowers surrounding our name with deep sadness, remembering a beautiful time before our family had been ripped apart.

I entered the house, listening for the sounds of children. Hearing none, I assumed that Gracie and Jack were still with our friends.

"Dad, I'd like to see the kids."

With compassion in his eyes, he nodded and headed up the stairs to my office to call the neighbor who had been watching them. I walked heavily to the couch and sat down. Each breath was short and I fought to keep from collapsing with emotion. There would be time for that later. Just one and a half, Jack was too little to understand what was happening. But Gracie had just turned four and I knew I had to tell her immediately, before she heard of Cyndi's death from someone else.

My mind wandered listlessly. I felt as if I were walking a tightrope of dull shock, across the black abyss of reality. I could feel icy fingers of pain reaching for me, but for now a sense of numbness was stronger than my emotions. I looked around the room, not really focusing on anything. Each small noise seemed to come from miles away. I was aware of deep emotion and sadness, but the pain wasn't as crushing as I would have expected. How long I sat there motionless, I don't know. Suddenly, the sound of the doorbell caused me to stir.

Slowly, as if in a dream, I walked over and opened the door. Big Dave was looking down, nervously flipping his baseball hat in his hands. When he looked up, I could see that his eyes were red. Neither of us exchanged a greeting. He simply walked through the doorway and sat down next to me on the stairs. We sat together in awkward silence, stunned and in disbelief: intimate friends with nothing to say. Time seemed to stand still. Outside the window, the sun appeared suspended in the blue sky, as if the night might never come.

Then a blur of activity streaked by the etched glass near the front door. My heart sank as I recognized Gracie's voice. Seconds later, she burst in wearing her usual, gregarious smile. With intuition beyond her years, she stopped abruptly upon seeing Dave and me motionless on the stairs. She raised her eyebrows and lowered her chin at an angle, as if to say that she knew we were up to something.

Dave quickly took his cue and walked into the kitchen.

Straightening, I took Gracie's little hand and walked a few feet into the living room. In the corner was a giant leather chair that Cyndi had given me for my thirtieth birthday. It seemed an appropriate place to talk with Gracie.

I sat down on the ottoman and faced her, holding her by the waist. Summoning every ounce of strength I had, I determined that

I wouldn't make this more difficult for her with a huge display of emotion.

"Gracie, this is going to be really hard to understand but I want you to listen to me," I said in a voice that sounded far calmer than I felt.

Amazingly, she kept eye contact and remained still. I pressed on.

"Jesus loves Mommy very, very much and He took her home to heaven. Gracie, Mommy was very sick and she died. We're not going to see her for a long time. But, we *will* see her again in heaven. Jesus loves you, Mommy loves you, and Daddy loves you very much."

"Mommy's not coming home today?" Her voice quivered and her eyes welled with tears.

"No, honey. Mommy isn't coming home for a while. But Daddy and Grandma Marty will take care of you."

She stepped back and began to whimper. My mom hurried in from the kitchen, gathered her in her arms and quickly left the room. With great wisdom, my mom kept Gracie close to her while she went to pick up Jack at a friend's house, then took both children back to her place to avoid the inflow of people that she knew were sure to come to our home.

Now that I had told Gracie, the flood of emotion overtook me. I covered my face with my hands and groaned with pain, tears falling freely onto the leather ottoman that had been a gift from my bride.

A great number of family and friends made their way in and out of the house that afternoon, each one giving me a brief hug before retreating to the painful quiet of the house. Most of the time I sat alone on the couch, feeling unsettled by the whispers and hushed activity in the kitchen behind me.

Everything had happened so quickly. Less than twenty-four hours earlier, Cyndi and I were swimming in the pool of our hotel in Hawaii. Just that morning, Cyndi and I talked and held hands at the airport. *How could she be gone? How could this have happened so fast?* My mind was racing, trying to make sense out of a collapsing world. *Jesus, help me. I need You.*

From my vantage point, I could watch the front door open each time someone new came into the house. Every time someone looked my way, the dagger of pain was forced deeper into my chest. Each person represented a special time of life for Cyndi and me, a special relationship. As each one appeared, the wound tore open just a little larger as I had to acknowledge that those days were over.

When Ryan walked through the door I rose and shook his hand as he put his arm around my back. We both sobbed deeply and Ryan's grip tightened as he tried to impart courage and communicate loyalty to me.

As the evening progressed, acquaintances left for home while close friends and family gathered in the living room.

Greg Stier arrived that night from Florida and we wept together over the loss of Cyndi. Realizing that everyone had gathered, I asked Greg to lead us in some kind of a devotional.

It was one of the few times in his life when I saw Greg hesitant. Moved by great emotion, Greg opened his Bible and read the story of Jesus and Lazarus.

"Right now, I don't have any answers, and I don't know if I ever will," he admitted. "But I do know that when Jesus learned of Lazarus' death, He wept. Jesus knows what we're experiencing here tonight and He hears our cries of pain. He has not forgotten us. And let's remember, after He wept, He raised Lazarus from the grave!"

We closed in prayer and people began gathering their things to leave. I lingered near a few of my friends but remained completely oblivious to their conversation. Emotion began to well up inside me as I realized I was avoiding going up to bed. I didn't want to sleep in the bed Cyndi and I had shared for the past seven years, knowing she wouldn't be there.

I left my friends in the kitchen and walked around the corner to the staircase. It might as well have been Mt. Everest, the eleven steps appeared so steep and foreboding. I began to crawl up the steps. Pathetically, I scratched my way on all fours to the top and nearly fell into our bedroom.

I closed the door behind me, stumbled toward the bed, and collapsed into the fetal position in the place where Cyndi usually slept.

The next few days were a blur. I wandered the house like a ghost, seeing and hearing but completely unable to touch or connect in any way to the people around me.

On the third day, I walked into my walk-in closet to get ready for the memorial service. Caring family members had made sure my dress clothes were pressed and my shoes shined. Methodically, I began to dress surrounded by Cyndi's clothes, each one bringing a different memory.

To my utter frustration, I was unable to button my shirtsleeves. I hadn't eaten in days and my hands were clumsy and jittery. After trying repeatedly, I slunk against the wall in defeat.

When I looked up I saw the tall form of my friend Craig Rants in front of me. Craig and I had been basketball teammates in high school and had become close friends over the years. Without a word, he buttoned both shirtsleeves and put a hand on my back as I walked out of my room and down the stairs to the waiting limousine.

Twenty minutes later the long, black car slowed to a stop under the awning of the mortuary. I opened the door, my heart pounding at the sight of people lining the hallway before me. As I made my way through the maze of people, they expressed their condolences one by one, usually with a nod or a pat on the shoulder.

As I walked through the hallway, I recognized my music coming from an inner room in the mortuary and I knew Cyndi would be in there. I caught the attention of Ryan and Dave, who were standing in the corner.

"Why are they playing my music?" I asked incredulously.

"I knew you wouldn't want that. But, hey, I'm not going to be the one to turn it off." Dave smiled.

I looked around the room and was encouraged by the presence of close friends and family members who I knew shared my deep sense of loss. My heart felt somewhat lighter as I realized that I wasn't the only one carrying the burden this day.

In an adjoining room, Cyndi lay peacefully among the flowers sent by those who loved her. People cleared out of the way as I approached, as if Moses was parting the Red Sea.

I had dreaded the moment when I would see her in this context: made up, stiff, lifeless. But somehow, I found a strange comfort in looking upon her. Her hair had been combed and styled, but it wasn't how she would have done it. Her makeup had been applied to appear like it did in Cyndi's pictures, but the amount seemed excessive compared to her usual simple tastes. Everything about her appearance was well done, but not *real*. Her signature smile — the essence of who she was — was gone and, with it, everything I loved about Cyndi.

This wasn't Cyndi, this was her earthly shell. The Cyndi I loved was now rejoicing in the presence of God and the angels.

Bending down, I kissed her forehead three times.

"This is for Jack."

"This is for Grace."

"And, this is for me. We love you Cyndi."

With that, I left the room.

A calm wind blew across the muted gray sky. After the graveside service, a small group of about fifty people crossed the yellow winter grass on their way back to their cars. After leaving the cemetery, the slow procession came to a stop at Cherry Hills Community Church on the southern edge of Denver.

Inside the church, close family and friends gathered upstairs. Large trays of food had been prepared and I was reminded by more than one person to make sure I ate something to keep up my strength. I didn't. I couldn't. After this small gathering and a word of prayer, we walked toward the main sanctuary. Standing outside the closed doors, my mom reached down and grabbed my hand. Following suit, my sister Susie reached over and held my other hand. Someone opened the doors and Greg led my family and me down the center aisle toward the front of the sanctuary.

I looked around, awestruck. The church was nearly filled. Fifteen hundred people had come to honor Cyndi and support her family. Beautifully haunting strains of piano filled the auditorium. As I took a seat I looked up and caught a nod from my friend Fernando Ortega. The Spirit of God was moving in that room more powerfully than I had ever experienced it. Both sorrow and understanding seemed to fall upon the congregation from above.

The service opened to the sound of muffled sobs and choked voices. One by one, family members walked to the platform to share stories of how unique and meaningful Cyndi's life had been.

The night before I had prepared a statement of sorts, though I was not then sure I would have the physical strength to deliver it. Following the lead of God, which I felt in my spirit, I nodded to my dad on the platform to indicate that I'd like to speak. Somehow I made it up the stairs, then gripped the podium and read through my tears.

Sweet Cyndi,

My cup is overflowing. God in His goodness lavished upon us a life together that neither of us could have imagined on that cold November night so long ago. Grace and beauty showered our existence as we spent the last fifteen years together.

You were all I ever knew. I am daunted by the thought of expressing our lives in a few short paragraphs. There were so many wonderful experiences we shared. There were so many layers to our relationship and love affair. Though many secrets will be kept in the vault of my soul, these are a few snapshots that I will treasure whenever I think of them.

You laughed. Your joy was effervescent and contagious. I remember the night we met somewhere near Monument, Colorado, at a youth group progressive dinner. I spilled ice cream on you and you laughed as if you enjoyed it. I remember passing notes, and secret kisses between passing periods in high school. I remember writing horrendously awful songs for you as I began to play guitar, and putting them on tape so everyone could hear. I remember wanting to rent a Cookie Monster outfit for the prom because the costume shop was cheaper than tuxedo rental and watching your face as I broke the exciting news. I also remember how astonishing you looked when I picked you up that night. You were unforgettable in white lace, even if you did have to ride in a Ford Pinto. Thank God your dad let us trade for his Mercedes.

I remember walking around the campus at Colorado State talking and dreaming of our lives together. We were young, in love, and full of life. The night I asked you to marry me was full of drama and excitement. You screamed, you covered your face, and then you kissed me. Our wedding day was a blur of flowers and friends. I remember the flowers you held in your hands as you looked up shyly as I entered the bridal room to view my bride. On that sacred and beautiful spring day, we committed our lives to one another in a celebration that only you could have planned.

There are few images in my mind more precious than the day Grace was born. After a difficult delivery, Gracie was first presented to us in the wee hours of the morning. As the nurse gently laid her next to your side, the morning light captured your face in ways I will always remember. You overflowed with love. It was more than physical; there was a spiritual depth to your tenderness. It was if you were hugging and squeezing that little girl with your eyes. Once again your mercy led us into adoption. As we drove baby Jack home from the hospital, I don't think he had any idea that his new mommy wasn't going to let him out of her arms for the world. Cyndi, you cherished that boy more than your own life.

Sweet and devoted wife, mother of two wonderful children for all of eternity, loving daughter, faithful sister, caring aunt, and lover of the broken, I have spent the last couple of days searching my soul. I have asked the question why and I have been grieved to the point of physical exhaustion. But I find that very short-lived. You left me full and satisfied. Where some may feel a hole, I have a deep, deep well filled by your warm spirit of servanthood and devotion. In the years to come, I will draw from that strength and peace as I raise our children. We shared an unbelievably wonderful life together. God, in His grace, gave us so much time together to travel, to love, and to grow as a family. Not a week went by that we didn't look at one another and thank God for what He had given us. I am so thankful, I am so thankful, I am so thankful. I am so undeniably blessed. I rejoice in your life and I rejoice in the memories of our love. Your essence is emblazoned on our children and your legacy will serve to guide and encourage

them as they grow in godliness. You embodied hope.
You lived compassion and your life will bring honor to
God in ways you could never have imagined. I will love
you with everything that I am, forever.

P.S. I know in heaven there is no need for marriage —
that we will be fulfilled by Christ. But I do believe there
will be a tunnel going from my mansion to yours.

Then I took my seat and drank in the ministry of the Holy Spirit
as Fernando sang "Give Me Jesus."

In the morning when I rise
In the morning when I rise
In the morning when I rise
Give me Jesus
Give me Jesus
Give me Jesus
You can have all this world
Give me Jesus
And when I come to die
Oh, when I come to die
And when I come to die
Give me Jesus

That song would echo through my head many times a day as the
hand of God began to heal our family.

Again, God was moving. This time, I would hear a whisper that
would change my life in ways I could never have anticipated.

Cyndi in Guatemala, meeting our sponsor child, Estella, for the first time.

12

The Whisper

THE DAY AFTER THE FUNERAL, I HUDDLED ON THE COUCH WITH A BLANKET. Outside the window, white skies grew even thicker with clouds as a winter storm blew over the mountains into Denver. The hours passed but I remained physically and mentally motionless, the weight of grief pinning me to the couch.

Snow began to fall, gently laying a blanket of white over the yard, the trees, and the sidewalk, dampening every sound. The house was eerily quiet. The first few days after Cyndi's death, the phone had rung nonstop. In contrast, the phone now was silent as people tried to give me space. But I didn't want space. Sometimes I wanted someone to talk with, to cry with. At other times, I didn't. The fact was, I wasn't sure what I wanted.

Grace and Jack had spent the previous night at Grandma Marty's, so the only noise was that of my Aunt Ruthie. She was organizing sympathy cards with what she hoped was mute precision, but somehow the effort to work quietly simply made her movements seem all the more pronounced and hellaciously loud.

A loud knock broke the monotony. Moving lethargically, I opened the front door and saw a man dressed in UPS brown, his breath rising to vapor in the cold air.

"I've got a lot of boxes for you. Where would you like me to put them?"

I knew exactly what was in them. "Um, I'll open the garage and help you get them in there."

It was the morning of Friday, February 8. The CD that Cyndi and I had invested so much of our lives in had finally arrived. Months earlier, I had scheduled a CD release party for Sunday night, February 10. Hundreds of posters had been tacked up around all over Colorado weeks before the event. On Monday, the day Cyndi had died, thousands of promotional mailings for the concert and the new record had arrived in mailboxes around the country. As people received their invitation to the concert, many went to my website for details, only to read the terrible news about Cyndi.

During the week, I had questioned God's timing. *God, why make everything so dramatic? Why would you take Cyndi home on the very day everyone received a mailing for the concert?* But over time, and through much prayer, God would reveal His great sovereignty and love. In time, I would see how He had used that postcard to prepare the church to pray for and support our family.

The UPS truck pulled away into the driving snow while my hands, numb with cold, worked to open the first box. In a moment, I found myself looking at thirty CDs bearing the title *Nothing Left to Prove.*

I took one out of the box and headed up to my room. As I shut the door, a folded piece of yellow paper fell to the ground from the open CD. I picked up the paper and turned it over. Staring back at me was a picture of Cyndi.

Back when we were planning the assembly of the CDs, I had asked Compassion International if I could include an insert that would tell people how they could sponsor needy children from around the world. After visiting many of these children overseas with Compassion over the last few years, Cyndi and I both felt strongly about the importance of Compassion's ministry. For Cyndi, loving hurting children was the essence of Christian life.

I had forgotten that each CD would be carrying a Compassion insert. Cyndi's picture took me completely by surprise. There she was with her big smile, looking at one of our sponsor children from Guatemala, Estella. Predictably, her hands were wrapped around the little girl, showing that she was important, of immeasurable worth. It was an incredibly beautiful picture. It was so . . . Cyndi.

The picture remained on my nightstand for almost a year.

That weekend the storm drifted out to the prairies, leaving dustings of snow and cold temperatures in its wake. Sunday night came and went without the planned CD release concert.

Monday morning brought a fresh sense of pain. It had been one week since Cyndi died. Somehow, it still seemed as though she could walk through the door at any moment, holding a bag of groceries in her arms and sharing a story about Jack's latest antics. Each time the garage door opened, I was reminded that the person there wasn't Cyndi and the wound tore a little deeper.

As afternoon approached, I felt desperate to get out of the house, to move, to think.

I drove south under gray skies. Twenty miles north of Colorado Springs, I turned east off the highway toward Monument. I meandered through the back roads toward Cyndi's childhood home, hoping to access a memory that was tangible enough to make her seem near. But she wasn't there. Somehow in my desperation, I had felt that I might hear her laughter in the wind or sense her presence in the mountains of our youth and early love. But I heard no voice and felt no ghost. Instead of finding solace in reminiscence, I felt completely and utterly alone.

The wind blew cold through the pine trees that lined the deserted road. I have always loved the way the mountains make the evening sky turn purple as dusk approaches. But this night, the stars haunted me.

"Stop the car."

The random thought had somehow forced its way into my mind. I ignored it and continued to drive.

"Stop the car."

As if I had heard an audible voice, those three words reverberated in my mind. *I must be going crazy*, I thought. *It's cold out there. I must be really messed up if I'm hearing voices.*

The message became more insistent.

"Stop the car."

I had no idea what was going on. I decided that although I might be going crazy, perhaps I should listen just in case what I was hearing was the voice of God. *Okay*, I thought. *I don't get it, but I'll stop the car.*

I heard the lonely crunch of tires rolling over gravel as I slowed to a stop. Placing the car in park, I leaned forward until my head was resting on the steering wheel. A burning ache filled my stomach.

"Get out of the car and walk toward that hill."

By this time, I had resigned myself to hearing voices. I decided that at least I would have friends to keep me company on my trip to insanity.

I opened the door and walked across the empty road.

The quiet of February rested upon the mountains but a roar of pain was growing within my chest. Looking to the stillness and majesty of the hills for comfort, I found only the breath of the wind. My feet slid on the rocks as I climbed my way to the top of the small hill overlooking the valley.

Cyndi had hiked these hills as a girl, and we once had dreamed of building a house in these high mountain meadows, lush with the crisp scent of cold pine. But as I stood looking across the valley, those dreams seemed impossibly long ago. I wrapped my arms around myself and shivered in the wind as darkness fell.

What was I doing?

I remembered reading that people who had become lost in the wilderness during winter storms were often found frozen to death with their arms around the trunk of a tree. Desperately, they had wanted to cling to something, anything, with their last ounce of strength. Was I now so despondent that I'd followed an imaginary voice on the wind to a cold mountainside, wearing no jacket and searching for a sliver of hope or understanding?

Had I known definitely that what I was hearing was the voice of God, I would have passionately embraced every word. But pain and confusion muddled my thoughts and twisted my emotions.

I reached the top of the hill and stood there panting, overlooking the valley, lost in grief.

Then I heard the voice again, and its whisper reverberated through my body.

"She is not cold."

A great surge of emotion coursed through me, like a white-hot bolt of lightning across a summer sky.

I was not alone.

In the moment when I thought I truly had fallen apart, God

Almighty — the Creator and Sustainer of the universe — had come to me in a whisper on the winter wind. Validating my pain, His words had the effect of arms wrapped around me to hold together all of the broken pieces. God had joined me in my dark night of pain. He had brought me to this mountaintop to reveal to me His great love and understanding. To give me hope.

As I looked out across the valley, my mind raced wildly. I pictured Jesus kneeling in the Garden of Gethsemane — death and torment slinking in the shadows — asking the Father if the bitter cup of suffering could be taken from him. Then the gentle voice of God assured his Son that death was not the end, that the pain would pass, and that in its place would come glory and redemption.

Falling to my knees, I realized God was meeting me in the same way He had met Jesus on His own dark night. The promise was not that the suffering would be taken away, but that God had not forgotten me. He had not forgotten the anguish and suffering that accompanies death. He understood the crushing weight of grief. He had not forgotten the pain that comes from losing someone, and He would not leave me to suffer alone.

He would not forsake me.

He would not forsake my children.

He had not forsaken Cyndi.

When God whispered, "*She is not cold,*" He pointedly addressed my deepest shame as a husband: that I had been unable to protect Cyndi; that she was now alone and cold, away from her children, in a grave; and there was nothing I could do to comfort or love her.

As I looked down at my hands, red with cold, I could hear the echo of God's whisper.

"*She is not cold.*"

God was speaking of heaven: the stark contrast to life on earth. Glory. Joy. Reunion. Redemption. Jesus, face-to-face! Heaven.

Cyndi was not cold. She was not alone. She was in the presence of a God who had loved her since before the beginning of time. She was not in a grave on the outskirts of Denver. She was in heaven!

I lifted my head and wiped at my eyes. In the distance, cars on the highway began to flick on their headlights against the darkening sky. I was reminded of a passage in Revelation in which the apostle John writes that there is no need for a light source in heaven because Jesus illuminates the City of God.

"You don't need light, Cyndi!" I said, my voice breaking.

"You're not cold! You're not cold. . . . " My voice trailed off as emotion overtook me.

I pressed my hands against the frozen ground in front of me.

"You're no longer sick. Your body is no longer in pain. You made it! You're in heaven!"

"Thank you, Jesus," I wept sincerely.

I wanted to remain on that hill all night, thanking God for speaking to my soul. But my chattering teeth told me that it was time to rejoice inside the car.

I drove home filled with thoughts of heaven that made me feel alive again. I wondered if Cyndi had yet talked with my Grandpa, if she had met the child that had died in my mother's womb five months after conception, if she had talked with Moses or the apostle Paul. I wondered if she had asked Jesus why she'd needed to suffer through cancer or why He took her home early, before her children were grown. I imagined Cyndi pleading with Jesus to allow her to help the kids and me from heaven, knowing that I was incapable of using an iron, much less of raising children on my own. I also wondered if she knew how much her life had meant to those who knew her and if she had any idea how much she was already missed. Could she see us? Was there any way for me to communicate my love to her? The questions were endless.

This was just the beginning. The joy and incomprehensibility of heaven would soon permeate all of my thoughts and shape the way I viewed my existence not just in the afterlife, but on earth. And little Gracie was about to do something that would encourage thousands of lives, for years to come.

Cynthia Lyne Oertli

Born: *May 7, 1971 in Little Rock, Arkansas*
Passed Away: *February 4, 2002 Denver, Colorado*

Gracie, high atop the "lightning tree."

13

Mommy
PAINTS THE SKY

THE WEEK FOLLOWING CYNDI'S DEATH I HAD FELT LIKE I WAS HIKING IN a deep wood shrouded by dense fog, waiting for the sun to break a hole in the mist and illuminate a path out of the darkness. When God led me to the mountaintop near Cyndi's childhood home and spoke of heaven, I felt the first ray of light pierce my pain. But the road to healing would take much longer than one week.

For nearly a month, I did little more than sit in the living room while the kids played on the floor, my mind thousands of miles away. I wanted to connect, but was not able to.

My aunt, Ruthie, continued to train missionaries for The Navigators organization during the day. At night and on weekends, she put her personal life on hold and stayed at the house, diligently cleaning many of the messes the kids and I had made as well as organizing anything that may have been out of place. This was everything: school papers, sympathy cards, and mail to name a few. Most importantly, she took time to love the children.

Each night, she would dress in brightly colored African robes, as she had for many years as a missionary in Kenya. Gently, she would lay down with the children and tell them stories of God's faithfulness until the day's activities caught up with them and they drifted off to sleep. Her presence in our home provided clear stability for their confused little hearts, and God used her to minister to them in a way only a woman could.

"Ruthie, I can't tell you how grateful I am that you've been so willing to help me and the kids," I told her one night. "We are truly thankful. But, I know you have a life back in Colorado Springs. Maybe it's time for you to get back to that life. We'll be okay here." Though I said it, I seriously doubted that were true.

Ruthie looked away. "You know I've never had children," she said, her eyes welling with tears. "I believe God has allowed me the privilege of mothering Gracie and Jack in my old age."

As if to say *This conversation is over*, she rose to leave. "You're not going to get rid of me that easily," she said over her shoulder.

With her quick mind and devotion to God, Ruthie was a blessing not only to Grace and Jack, but to me as well. As the burden of grief became one I needed to share, Ruthie was present to listen. Most nights after the kids were asleep, we talked by the light of the fireplace in the family room. For nearly fifteen years, I had processed my thoughts and emotions by talking with Cyndi. Now that Cyndi was gone I felt stifled, bottled up. I wanted to share with someone all that was happening in my heart and mind. Ruthie's presence provided a much-needed transition in my life, helping me to practice sharing my deepest thoughts and feelings with people other than Cyndi.

During those early months, God created an amazing support group for the kids and me. Like Ruthie, my parents were constantly around the house. Tireless servants, they cared for the children that first year more than anyone else did, including myself. Second only to my mom's belief that food heals was her conviction that children need to be held. Whenever a problem arose, big or small, Gramma held the kids on her lap until the difficulty blew over. Strangely, that usually seemed to work.

My dad — or as Gracie liked to called him, "Crappa Jay"—helped me transition into running the business side of my music ministry, something Cyndi had always handled. Though I had performed concerts for years, I knew little about the office work that was done at home. Like Sherlock Holmes and his trusty sidekick Watson, my dad and I sifted through the computer files making notes until we were able to figure out Cyndi's systems of organization and accounting.

Most mornings, I would wake to find the kids dressed and ready for the day, my mom standing in the kitchen talking with Ruthie while my dad tried for the hundredth time to form a pancake into the shape of Mickey Mouse.

My sister's family lived less than a mile away and Grace and Jack spent many afternoons playing in the yard with their cousins. My high school basketball buddy and faithful friend Craig Rants also ministered to us by doing household chores and helping me to regain my smile through spirited games of ping-pong.

Cyndi's close friend Kate McRostie, an accomplished interior designer and artist, redecorated much of the house and chose new colors for each bedroom. Though it was difficult to change things that Cyndi had done, embracing the colors of a new world was for us an important step toward healing.

Big Dave remained connected by spending the night at our house every Monday night after his seminary class. Like me, Dave processed his thoughts verbally, and we often talked until the early hours of the morning. On many of those Mondays, Ryan made the long trek from his house in the mountains to join us, and I would awake the next morning to find the two of them asleep on the couches in the family room.

The long process of healing had begun. In some ways, I felt guilty. Many people who had lost a spouse or loved one were not blessed with a support system like the one that had developed around me. The Lord continually reminded me to remain grateful and to use this time to heal. I did my best, knowing that grieving now would make me a more effective and loving father in the future.

Leafing through the messages on my desk one night, I came across the name of Fran Sciacca. At the Christian High School in Colorado Springs that Cyndi and I had attended, Fran had been our Bible teacher. Since that time, he had moved to Birmingham to teach at another Christian School. After hearing about Cyndi's death, Fran had called to say that he was praying for my family and me. On a whim, I picked up the phone and dialed the number. After nearly an hour, I put down the phone and looked out the window into the darkness with a smile on my face.

What a wonderful, godly man.

Fran had great insight into people, but more importantly, Fran knew Scripture. As we continued to talk by phone each week, Fran carefully redirected my attention from secular wisdom to examples of faith and trust found in the Bible. He was concerned that I look to God and not to man for healing and understanding. It was Fran who showed me God's roadmap to healing found in Isaiah 58:6-12:

> Is not this the kind of fasting I have chosen: to loose the
> chains of injustice and untie the cords of the yoke, to set
> the oppressed free and break every yoke? Is it not to
> share your food with the hungry and to provide the

poor wanderer with shelter — when you see the naked,
to clothe him, and not to turn away from your own flesh
and blood? Then your light will break forth like the
dawn, and your healing will quickly appear; then your
righteousness will go before you, and the glory of the
LORD will be your rear guard. Then you will call, and
the LORD will answer; you will cry for help, and he will
say: Here am I. . . . The LORD will guide you always; he
will satisfy your needs in a sun-scorched land and will
strengthen your frame. You will be like a well-watered
garden, like a spring whose waters never fail. Your
people will rebuild the ancient ruins and will raise up
the age-old foundations.

The language of this passage was so poetic and compelling, I felt as
if God were speaking directly to me. It is easy to get caught up in the
whirlpool of self-absorption and self-pity, and I had allowed myself to
swim in those dangerous waters. Through Fran and Isaiah, God was
teaching me to take my eyes off myself and focus on others. It would be
a hard-fought battle, as everything in me wanted to pull back from
people and wallow in suffering.

During those early weeks, Ruthie brought home a devotional
book by Joni Eareckson Tada, called *Heaven: Your Real Home*. I soon
found myself fervently praying for the Lord's return almost hourly. I
became consumed with thoughts of heaven and Jesus. Though I still
ached with pain, God had begun to fill the void in my spirit with a
desire to know Him more. I read most of the Christian books I could
get my hands on and listened to sermons on tape while driving in the
car. For the first time in my life, I had an insatiable desire to really

know God. As during Cyndi's cancer treatment years, pain again had stripped away the pretense in my life. I wanted only what was real and lasting: God. When I was weary and in pain, the only thing that brought me comfort was thoughts of Jesus and His mercy.

God continued to heal me emotionally during the following months, and I began to regain physical strength as well. Over a period of six weeks, I had lost almost fifteen pounds, some of my hair had fallen out, and — though no one took me seriously — I truly thought my fingernails had stopped growing.

Believing that there is a direct correlation between recovery and chocolate chips, my mom primed the pump of my appetite by keeping a container of cookies on the kitchen counter. With this steady diet of sugar and flour, it wasn't long before those fifteen pounds found their way back onto my body and my fingernails suddenly needed a manicure. And, of course, as everyone knows, cookies lead to pizza and pizza leads to healthy eating — at least in the home I grew up in.

Despite this flawed nutritional logic, I was getting better. But with renewed physical strength came restlessness. I needed to get away from the house that had held me captive for six weeks. I also needed to again pursue the ministry God had called me to: music.

In March, I boarded the plane to Tennessee surrounded by Dare2Share friends, including Greg Stier, who had become as close as family. From Denver, we flew to Chicago's O'Hare airport for a layover. At the airport food court, I watched the people around me hurrying about and talking in what seemed to be unusually loud voices. For weeks, I had lived my life away from the bustle of people and without the sensory stimulation of television. Now I sat in wonderment, taking in the frenetic pace and noise of the American lifestyle. My world had stopped, but for everyone else life continued as usual.

The following day, I prepared to lead the band in a twenty-minute worship set at East Tennessee State University. Less than a minute before show time, I felt Greg's hand on my shoulder. "Hey man, just do what you can," he said, his faced etched with concern. "If you need to end early, we'll figure it out."

His understanding was comforting. Seconds later I took a deep breath and walked onto the stage, surrounded by my brothers and sisters in Christ.

The next twenty minutes were amazing. Though my voice was tired and out of shape, the joy of worshiping God overwhelmed me. The deep thud of the kick drum grooved with the bass guitar behind me, and it felt healing to once again sling my guitar over my shoulder.

The following week, Ruthie gave me a sermon on tape given by her pastor in Colorado Springs. The message revolved around King David and his response to pain. Moved by the pastor's words, I picked up my Bible and read Psalms 41–42. David was no stranger to grief and suffering, and his lament to the Lord was compelling. Time and again in these two chapters David resolutely stated, "Put your hope in God. For I will yet praise Him!" It seemed as if David was girding himself against the onslaught of pain, forcing himself to dispel his weakness and put his faith in God. In David I found a fellow journeyman who may not have understood everything God was up to, yet continued to follow Him in faith.

I then realized that worship is sometimes based on faith, not joy, and that some of our most sincere times of worship are conducted through tears. For the first time since Cyndi's death, I picked up my guitar to write a song.

Worship You with Tears

You know when I rise
You know when I sleep
You know that I need You desperately
I pour out my soul, oh Lord
I worship You with tears
I am broken
I have nothing to give
I fall at Your feet
And worship You with tears
Where can I go
To meet with You Lord
My soul is so thirsty for You
Send forth Your truth, as I
Worship You with tears
(chorus)

WORDS AND MUSIC BY DANNY OERTLI (MAY, 2002)

Summer arrived and I did my best to take every opportunity to spend time with my children. Many days, we would venture into the field across from our house to sit upon the Great Lightning Tree and talk about life — or life as seen through the eyes of a four-year-old and an almost-two-year-old. The tree was a great cottonwood from years past that had been knocked horizontal by a bolt of lightning. The kids seemed to believe it was a magical place and I did nothing to discourage them. It was our haven, our secret place to go as a family, another place for God to heal and bond us through laughter and dreams.

As fall descended upon the Rocky Mountains, Gracie traveled with me to Alaska, where I was to lead worship for a family conference. One night as I slept, I stepped outside and found myself staring up at the majestic Aurora Borealis. In all my life, I had never seen anything so beautiful, so surreal. In wide-eyed wonder, I gazed at the colorful theater that was the northern sky. The colors swirled from silvery blue to green, with an occasional burst of pinkish red on the horizon.

Slowly, the awe I felt turned to introspection. *If God can light the forest with the surreal beauty of dancing lights, how much more can He help me walk this lonely road of pain? If He controls the heavens, what am I so afraid of?*

It would not be the last time God encouraged me with the magnificence of His creation.

One month later, Grace, Jack, and I were driving down the road in my really fast Honda minivan. As we pulled into a parking space at Wal-Mart an incredible sunset began to form over the mountains. The car's interior was bathed in amber light and deep strokes of yellow crisscrossed the sky, as if drawn by an unseen hand.

"Daddy," came Gracie's little voice from the back seat, "Did God let mommy paint the sky tonight?"

Looking in the rearview mirror I saw her leaning into Jack to catch a better view. As the light from the sunset settled on their faces, I silently praised God for the healing and hope that He had brought into our lives.

For months, I had been assuring Gracie and Jack that God had not forgotten us and that He loved us more than we could imagine. I had used big words like "sovereign" and "eternity," concepts even I didn't understand. But with the brush of His hand, God spoke to Gracie that night in a way I could not.

With thanksgiving for God's mercy, I wrote this song for Gracie:

Mommy Paints the Sky

JOB 26:13-14, PSALM 19:1

The wind blows your hair
On this warm November night
Your small hand in mine
And eyes that ask me why
But I don't know
But somewhere in the sky
Beyond the mountain peaks
The moon will find its voice
As the sun lays down to sleep
You ask me why she's gone
I don't know where to start
As the sunset lights your face
I see God knows how to heal little hearts

So He has
Mommy paint the sky
With deep ocean blue
She swirls the clouds red
To dance just for you
Mommy paints the sky
With the laughter of God
There by Jesus side
So high above

As if to say it won't be long
Mommy paints the sky

The heavens flame with gold
Slowly changing hue
The brilliance of a stage
That was made to shine for you
And with each amber flare
You watch her hand at play
Tender kisses fall
As she paints what words could never say

(chorus)
I'm so thankful
The heavens still proclaim
Mercy and healing
In the middle of the pain
So thank you Jesus
For keeping hope alive
With the beauty of heaven
Painted on an autumn sky
As if to say it won't be long
Mommy paints the sky

WORDS AND MUSIC BY DANNY OERTLI (JANUARY, 2003)

None of us knew it at the time, but I would sing that song hundreds of times and tell Gracie's story of hope and faith to countless people.

But God was not finished writing. There was another dramatic chapter to add to our story, and it would unfold much sooner than anyone expected.

Rayna, Danny, Jack, and Gracie, in the shadow of Pikes Peak.

14

$\mathcal{L}ive$ for

HEAVEN

ON THE ONE-YEAR ANNIVERSARY OF CYNDI'S DEATH, I AWOKE TO THE giggles of two small children. Rubbing the sleep from my eyes, I pushed myself up on my elbows and peeked over the side of the bed.

A devious-looking Gracie was whispering something in Jack's ear as they knelt on the floor. Not wanting to spoil their surprise, I quietly eased my head back onto the pillow and closed my eyes.

Seconds later, both of them jumped up and pounded on the bed with their hands.

"Wake up, Daddy! Wake up, Daddy!"

Usually, Jack alone rose early enough to alert the rooster that it was time to crow. But for some reason, both kids had awakened this morning and decided it was time to force me into daddyhood.

I had wanted this to be an intimate day with the children and me, so I had told my parents and Ruthie that I wanted to spend the morning alone with them. At the breakfast table, I asked them, "If you could do anything today, what would you want to do?"

Gracie wasted no time thinking it over. "Go sledding!"

Jack's eyes darted back and forth as he tried to remember what sledding was. With forced excitement he parroted his sister: "Thledding!" But I could tell he still had no idea what that was.

After spending nearly half an hour searching for boots, gloves, and snow bibs, we shoved all our gear into the minivan and drove to the park. Grace and Jack hopped out of the van into snow that came up to their knees. Immediately, Grace took charge and "helped" Jack get situated in the "thled." For the next two hours, I pulled them up and down the small hills around the park as we played, laughed, and made snow angels.

After a while, they each put one hand on the rope of the sled and walked toward an untouched section of snow on the other side of a field. Enjoying the rest, I watched them ramble off.

They had grown so much in the past year, Cyndi would hardly recognize them now. Oh, how I ached to tell her all that God had done to minister to these little children and to me. I ached to talk with her, to be with her, to once again share life with her.

Yet I had come to realize that beneath my yearning to be with Cyndi again was a deeper, more intense longing — an ancient song that had been echoing through my soul since the day I was born. It was a melody that had called to me as I lay beneath crabapple blossoms as a boy, drawing me into the endlessness of the night sky. It was the same voice that had groaned with words beyond hearing as I grieved the loss of my closest friend and companion. It was the voice of the composer who had whispered encouragement to me on a Colorado mountainside. It was the laughter of an artist whose brilliant colors could light up the northern sky — a voice that continually whispered, "*I love you. I am all you need.*"

The song I was drawn to — the longing in my heart — was for intimacy. Intimacy with Jesus.

That is why I had been so encouraged by thoughts of heaven. I had come to realize that heaven is all about Jesus, and we were created to be with Him. For only in Him do we find peace from suffering, love in pain, hope where there is desperation.

I glanced down at my watch. It was 10:30 A.M., the exact time Cyndi had died one year earlier. Looking up to heaven I prayed. *I still don't have it all figured out, God, and I'm going to need a lot more help. But thank you, Jesus. Thank you, Jesus. Come soon.*

⌒

May 29, 2003, was an incredibly beautiful spring day. It was also what would have been the ninth wedding anniversary for Cyndi and me.

Ever the faithful friend, Ryan had invited me up to his camp in the mountains for a morning of fishing. It seems as though guys are much more willing to talk if they can look at something — in this case, at a mountain stream — and not directly at one another, and Ryan knew it. Located just seven miles north of Woodland Park, Colorado, Quaker Ridge Camp is filled with rolling hills where Grace and Jack could explore with Ryan's wife, Julie, and their two little girls.

With the kids in good hands, Ryan and I waved good-bye and drove into the morning sun. Within minutes, we found ourselves meandering down a dirt road lined with tall pine trees. Ryan smirked as we passed a No Trespassing sign, then parked in a grassy space near a pristine mountain creek.

"Can we fish here? The sign said private property," I asked.

Ryan's bad boy act immediately disappeared. "Actually, I know the guy. He said we could fish here today."

We pulled on our waders, grabbed our fly rods and wicker creels, and eased our way through the bushes into the creek.

Ryan headed downstream as I eyed a dark pool of water swirling in the shade of a large boulder. Surely there was a large fish lurking in the depths of this hole. As a boy, my dad had taught me to cast for the rock, letting the fly drop more naturally into the water rather than swatting the surface with fishing line.

After a few rusty casts, I managed to drop the fly exactly where I wanted it. It rolled down the rock and gently glided along the water's surface.

I held my breath in anticipation.

Nothing.

I had learned another thing from my dad: One rarely catches a fish with the perfect cast; that would be too easy. Fish would rather string a person along.

I tried for a few minutes more but nothing stirred in the dark water. Almost as an afterthought, I decided to cast one final time before moving to another hole. To my surprise, my fly suddenly disappeared beneath the surface as the white belly of a trout flashed in the water, snatching the bait.

He was small, but he was going in my freezer. I'd been skunked too many times to go home empty-handed again.

Ryan joined me a while later and we each opened our creels for the other to inspect. Thankfully, his luck had been similar to mine. Neither of us had a right to gloat. In fact, the only rights we may have had were Miranda Rights — and it would have been wise to claim our "right to be silent" if we had been caught by the game warden with such small fish.

We sat down on the bank of the river to enjoy the setting. The stream bubbled in the background. We idly talked about his job as a camp director and about how music ministry was treating me. We laughed at a few old stories that we had told hundreds of times, but they had never seemed to lose their freshness. A pause reached our conversation and Ryan seized the moment. He broke the silence with a bang.

"Do you think you'll ever date again?" He grinned and watched the sun on the water.

I considered the question. God had done an immense amount of healing in my life, and for the past few weeks, I had felt that He was preparing me for something unexpected. Still, the idea of dating seemed foreign.

"I don't know. If lightning struck and it was the perfect situation, *maybe* I'd consider it."

Two months later, lightning struck.

~

Youth For Christ's DCLA evangelism training conference was one of the largest Christian youth events in the world. My job that summer was to travel to the District of Columbia to lead worship for the staff in the morning and host a coffee shop at night.

Lugging my guitar, I fought my way through the mass of kids moving through the Washington, D.C. Convention Center on the first night of the conference. The green room where artists prepared was stage left, cordoned off from the audience by black curtains. I held up my backstage pass for the security staff, pulled back the curtain, and entered to see a small group of people getting ready for the main session.

Near the stage entrance, I spotted Christian recording artist Geoff Moore. A good friend, Geoff had graciously asked me to join him for a few songs that night before ten thousand kids. We huddled near the stage stairs as he and his guitarist, Dana, reviewed for me the keys and chord progressions of the songs we would be playing.

Minutes before we were to go on stage, the curtain to the green room was pulled back and two women entered. As they approached us, I recognized one of them as my friend Suzie Johnson. Suzie worked in artist relations for Compassion International and had been my representative to that ministry for a few years.

"Hey, guys, ready to go?" she asked jovially.

"Suzie Johnson!" Geoff reached over and gave her a hug.

"Hey, I know you're about to go on. I just wanted to introduce you to Rayna. She's a new Compassion employee."

The room was dark and I was distracted by the thought of playing three songs I had never performed before in front of such a large crowd. I reached out and shook the woman's hand. My mind registered that I had just met a beautiful girl, but that information was quickly filed away as Geoff led the way up the stairs and onto the stage.

The following morning I arrived at the convention center early to lead a time of worship for the DCLA staff. When I had finished, I packed up my gear and began to make my way through the maze of halls, back toward my hotel room.

Out of the corner of my eye, I spotted a Compassion International display that was clearly in great distress. The support rods that were supposed to hold the giant nylon display in place were now sagging, causing the faces of the beautiful Compassion children to twist and distort like images in a circus mirror.

An old friend of mine, Kelley Erickson, was fighting a losing battle as she attempted to straighten the rods. I chuckled. Although I was mechanically inept I still wanted to help, so I made my way over to the table and offered my meager assistance. After a bit of work, Kelley and I somehow righted the display and the beautiful faces of the children again lit up the hallway.

Just then a slender girl with short, jet-black hair stepped out from around the display. My first impression was that she was like a deer, graceful and lithe, moving just slow enough to appear almost cautious.

As she and Kelley talked, my curiosity drew me closer.

Kelley politely introduced us. "Danny, this is Rayna. She just started with Compassion."

Realizing this was the same girl I had met the night before, I made an attempt at witticism, "Oh yeah, we go way back."

For the first time, I actually saw Rayna. Her face was thin, sculpted, with high cheekbones. Her eyes were of the deepest mahogany and appeared moist and gentle.

She smiled and said something back — I can't remember what. Then she turned to ask Kelley a question. I stood there, watching, as they conversed.

Wow, those are nice lips.

"Want to go to breakfast?" I blurted out, a complete non sequitur.

Remarkably, they said yes, and that morning Rayna learned that I like to eat my pancakes with my hands because they taste better that way. When I returned to my hotel room that evening, I stared into the mirror and shook my head.

What is going on?

It was the first time I had felt this way about a girl since the day I met Cyndi.

The emotions I had were intense, but confusing. I felt a strong sense of disloyalty over having feelings for a woman besides Cyndi. At the same time the thoughts of Rayna that had been racing through my mind all day were exhilarating.

The next day, I again happened by the Compassion booth. Rayna and Kelley were about to take a break and asked me to join them for lunch in the convention center food court.

As we were walking down the hallway, I turned to Rayna. "I knew a girl in elementary school named Raini," I said, "but I've never met a Rayna. What's your last name?"

"Cloud," she replied with quick smile. Suddenly, her eyes grew wide. "I mean ... Clark. It's ... Clark." She doubled over in embarrassed laughter.

As she fought to regain composure, I smiled at the way she pressed her tongue against the roof of her mouth and her upper teeth when she laughed, making an endearing *hnnn, hnnn, hnnn* sound.

She was obviously flustered. *Maybe she feels something too. Man, this is so new and strange.*

Yet she was so real.

I was in deep. This was going to take some prayer.

After five sleepless nights, I returned home from D.C. As always, the kids mauled me upon arrival and their display of affection left me bruised and sleepy.

When they had gone to bed, I dialed Fran in Alabama.

After talking for nearly thirty minutes, I finally worked up the nerve to tell him.

"Fran, I met someone."

"I wondered if something was up! There was something different in your voice tonight. Well, brother ... tell me about her."

Fran and I spoke late into the evening. I had so many questions about what was happening in my heart. I didn't know how to ask a girl out. I never really even asked Cyndi out. We just kind of ... started dating. What would Rayna think of my two kids? What would my kids think of her? Was this all too early? What would other people think?

The questions seemed endless.

In his gentle way, Fran encouraged me to pray about what the Lord would have me do.

"If God leads you in this direction, I would suggest being very honest and up front with her. Anytime a man with two children asks a woman out, there is serious intention. She knows that and you know that. Respect her and be honest with her and leave it in the Lord's hands. You'll know if this is from God."

That night I lay awake in bed for several hours, earnestly praying that God would give me clear direction. I didn't want to be led by emotion no matter how strong. I wanted what God wanted, and I wanted to be sure I was hearing from Him and not simply following my heart.

The following evening, my parents took care of the children as I drove my 1973 Ford Bronco — my desperate attempt to counteract the stigma of a minivan — to the southern foothills of Denver. Locking the hubs, I shifted into four-wheel drive and followed a dirt trail that led to the top of a mountain.

I arrived at the summit just in time to catch the sunset.

So many times in my life, God had used the beauty of His creation to inspire and speak to me. But this night, the assurance I felt in my heart would have been just as clear if I'd simply turned out the lights in my basement.

God was leading me to a beautiful girl who I knew nothing about. But after all that had happened, I knew I could trust Him.

In my mind, I placed my hand in His, asking Him to lead me.

With His other hand, He took the delicate fingers of a girl from California and slowly brought them toward mine.

Rayna and Danny, cutting the cake.

15

You Make

ME LOVE GOD

On Fran's advice, I asked Rayna out for ice cream a little more than a week after we met. My heart was beating fast, and I couldn't seem to shake the giddy smile that kept creeping onto my face as I drove south to Colorado Springs from Denver to pick her up at her apartment.

She was waiting for me as I pulled into the driveway and I thought of how proud my mom would be that I opened the car door for her to get in. A brilliant lightning storm was raging through the skies of Colorado Springs that night. While driving, I stole a glance her way just as a streak of whitish-blue lightning lit up her face. My heart dropped a beat at the sight of her beauty. I had already fallen in love with her kind and godly demeanor one week earlier in Washington, D.C. Now I found her physical beauty breathtaking: her delicate chin, her eyes wide and alive, gazing into the night. She was sitting on the very edge of her seat, the electricity between us mirroring the intense storm outside.

How had I come to this moment? *What am I doing?* I wondered. Yet in those brief seconds, for the first time I somehow sensed Cyndi's approval, and feelings of disloyalty began to dissolve as I thought of how much Cyndi would have loved Rayna's sweet spirit and caring attitude.

Even more important, I could sense God's approval. In all my life, I had never experienced anything so powerful, so compelling, so clearly from the Lord. To overcome any doubt, God was speaking specifically and boldly to each of us — leaving no question that this is what He intended.

It was a short drive and nothing of great significance was said, but the joy of heaven filled the car, and I felt an overwhelming sense of peace.

Rayna and I arrived at TGI Friday's and found a booth away from the crowds. We ordered chocolate shakes and talked for nearly a half an hour before I felt the time was appropriate to say something that I really should have prepared line by line, but of course had not.

"Rayna, I'm not sure how to say this and my deepest intention would be to never hurt you," I began. "But I'm coming out of a very difficult time and I want to be completely honest and up front with you. Actually, this isn't just for me. I'm kind of a package deal. I have two little carry-ons that come with me. Anyway, I don't really know how to say this, but . . . I think you're beautiful and I want to get to know you better."

"I'd like that, too." Rayna was trying to play it cool, but something in the way her eyes enlarged as I gave my speech told me she was as excited as I was.

The next day, Rayna came to the house to meet the kids. I had been careful not to burden them yet by telling them the significance of our relationship. Already, Gracie had been having difficulty at school knowing her family situation was different from some of the other children. On her first day of kindergarten, she asked the teacher not to tell the other students that she didn't have a mommy. Gracie longed for someone to fill that role in her life and I wanted to be cautious both with Rayna's emotions and with Gracie's. The kids believed she was just another friend who had come over to the house. But, man, did they leave a good first impression! If there was a handbook for impressing prospective mommies, Grace and Jack could have served as illustrations.

Immediately upon Rayna's entrance, Gracie took her hand and gave her a tour of the house. Within minutes, Jack had planted onto her lips a "squeeze kiss" — his invention whereby he squeezes the opposite party's lips into a line with his fingers and draws them toward him for a smooch. A bond was obviously forming — and far quicker than I would have imagined or hoped.

After a few hours of laughing and swinging in the back yard, Rayna prepared to leave. Gracie and Jack conspiratorially snuck outside and came back with flowers for Rayna to take with her.

Just before she drove away that evening, Ruthie turned to me and said, "That girl is pure gold. It's a miracle of God that she isn't married."

Over the next few weeks, it became obvious to both of us that we were going to get married sooner rather than later. Family and friends fell in love with Rayna as I had, seeing the joy she had brought to my life and our little family. One by one, they pulled me aside to give their sincere approval, hoping to learn our timetable for marriage. Everyone agreed that this was the work of a merciful and loving God. Eventually, Gracie caught on as well. One night, the three of us lay on the family room floor with Gracie in the middle watching a movie.

"Rayna, do you love my daddy?" she asked innocently.

"Yes, I do sweetie."

"Daddy, do you love Miss Rayna?"

I began to see where this was headed.

"Yes, I do Gracie," I said.

"Then why don't you marry her?" she concluded with a smile. With that, she took my hand and put it in Rayna's. It wouldn't be long.

More than once, the thought crossed my mind, *What would Cyndi think of all of this?* Of me remarrying? Of someone else raising the children? But there was always such an overwhelming sense of peace, those questions simply didn't haunt me as they could have. Instead, I pictured Cyndi giddy with excitement, looking down from heaven with joy in her heart at the love and stability Rayna was bringing to our home. The kids absolutely adored Rayna. Anytime Cyndi's name was mentioned, Rayna was affirming and loving, assuring Grace and Jack that Cyndi had left an incredible heritage for them of compassion and kindness and that she would never be forgotten.

If Cyndi could have searched the world for a woman to come into my life, love me, and raise the children she had cared for as babies, she would have picked Rayna.

Six months later, I prepared the room.

Behind a pillow on the leather chair near the fireplace, I had hidden a secret. Rayna walked into the family room and took her seat, awaiting her thirtieth birthday present.

I sat next to her, placed my guitar on my knee, and played this song.

You Make Me Love God

I can almost see the wink in His eye
On His throne up in heaven to an angel walking by
One by one He gathered them around
With His hand he moved the clouds aside
And with smiles they all looked down

And they clapped and danced

As I stole a glance

At this girl before my eyes

As I asked your name

An unheard serenade

Whispered through the skies

And somehow I knew

You make me

You make me

You make me love God

You make me

You make me

Oh, you make me love God

I can almost hear the joy in His sigh

As we walked under the moonlight

And you slipped your hand in mine

Stars sang their ancient melody

To the Maker of the heavens

Who brought you here to me

And in your face

I could see the grace

And the goodness of a King

With your head thrown back

I could hear in your laugh

All the angels sing

And I knew

(chorus)

There is so much more to love than emotion

So much more than chance

Love is heaven set in motion
God creates this dance
And just in case you only heard the melody
What I'm trying to say is . . .
Rayna, will you marry me

WORDS AND MUSIC BY DANNY OERTLI (NOVEMBER, 2003)

And God's song plays on, whispering truth through the pine trees, filling the heavens with laughter, encouraging His people that joy soon will replace suffering, and assuring us that heaven is not that far away.

Cyndi knows.

Live for heaven.

Resources

BOOKS AND SONGS THAT OFFER HOPE
FOR THOSE GRIEVING

BOOKS

Sittser, Gerald. *A Grace Disguised*. Grand Rapids, Mich.: Zondervan, 1998.

Lewis, C. S. *A Grief Observed*. San Francisco: Harper SanFrancisco, 1983.

White, Mary A. *Harsh Grief, Gentle Hope*. Colorado Springs: Navpress, 1995.

Tada, Joni Eareckson. *Heaven: Your Real Home*. Grand Rapids, Mich.: Zondervan, 1995.

Sprague, Billy. *Letter to a Grieving Heart: Comfort and Hope for Those Who Hurt*. Eugene, Ore.: Harvest House, 2001.

Vanauken, Sheldon. *A Severe Mercy*. San Francisco: Harper SanFrancisco, 1987.

Means, Dr. James. *A Tearful Celebration: Courage In Crisis*. Sisters, Ore.: Multnomah, 1985.

SONGS

"Faith To Be Strong," Andrew Peterson, Watershed Records, "Carried Along"

"Give Me Jesus," Fernando Ortega, Word Records, "Hymns of Worship"

"Hard to Get," Rich Mullins, Reunion Records, "The Jesus Demos"

"Hold Me Jesus," Rich Mullins, Reunion Records, "A Liturgy, A Legacy & A Ragamuffin Band"

"Joy," Dave Beegle, Hapi Scratch Records, "A Year Closer"

"Hallelujahs," Chris Rice, Rocketown Records, "Deep Enough to Dream"

"More Than Enough," Chris Thomlin and Louie Giglio, Sixsteps Records, "Not to Us"

"Nothing Is Beyond You," Rich Mullins, Reunion Records, "The Jesus Demos"

"The Silence of God," Andrew Peterson, Watershed Records, "Love and Thunder"

SONGS LYRICS INCLUDED IN THE BOOK:

"Four and 1/2 Months," *Hymns and Prayers*, 1999, Danny Oertli Music, ASCAP.

"She Sees Angels," Hymns and Prayers, 1999, Danny Oertli Music, ASCAP.

"Thought You Should Know," Nothing Left to Prove, 2002 Danny Oertli Music, ASCAP.

"Worship You with Tears," Live for Heaven, 2002 Danny Oertli Music, ASCAP.

"Mommy Paints the Sky," 2003, Danny Oertli Music, ASCAP.

"You Make Me Love God," 2004, Danny Oertli Music, ASCAP.

"Give Me Jesus," Fernando Ortega, 2002, Word Records.

About

THE AUTHOR

DANNY OERTLI IS AN ACCOMPLISHED SINGER AND SONGWRITER AND the father of two. His latest album, "Everything in Between," featuring the song "Mommy Paints the Sky," is a compilation of songs that reminds us of the faithfulness of God. Recently remarried, Danny and his wife, Rayna, live with Grace and Jack in Colorado.

Show compassion
to a child in poverty.

God can use you to bring love, hope and encouragement to a child living in extreme poverty. Through sponsorship, you'll be personally linked with a boy or girl who will know your name, write to you and treasure the thought that you care.

Your support of $28 a month provides opportunities for better health, vocational training, social development, safety and much more. The child you sponsor will also learn about Jesus and have regular interaction with Christians in a caring, church-based program.

Begin today! Your prayers, letters and friendship will mean so much to a child who really needs you!

Danny Oertli is a Compassion musician and currently sponsors seven children.